Sushi Secrets
A Japanese master's ultimate guide

text©2022 Seiichi Sakanishi
design©2022 Kazuhiko Tajima
photographs@2022 Hiroshi Yoda
©2022 PIE International

PIE International Inc.
2-32-4 Minami-Otsuka, Toshima-ku, Tokyo 170-0005 JAPAN
international@pie.co.jp
www.pie.co.jp/english

ISBN978-4-7562-5661-4 (Outside Japan)
Printed in Japan

鮨ネタ粋ワザ

Sushi Revealed:Secrets of a Japanese Chef

仕入れの極意

魚の仕入れは鮨の生命線だ。納得のいく魚をいかに仕入れるか。ここで味の大半は決まるため、毎日が真剣勝負である。市場に向かうのは早い日で深夜2時。競りが始まる前に魚を見繕い、仲買人と相談しながら意中のものを競り落としてもらう。たとえ数百尾の入荷があったとしても、買いたいと思えるのは10尾あるかないか。ひと握りの魚を買うために、誰よりも早く市場に行かねばならないのである。通う市場は豊洲がメインだが、横浜や川崎を回ることも少なくない。横浜の市場は東京湾の中でも横須賀や小柴などの魚に強く、川崎は平塚、茅ヶ崎、江の島など相模湾産が多く入る。そうやって上質の魚を揃えなければ、お客さまを唸らせることはできない。「この程度でいいか」という仕入れでは自分自身もつまらないのである。睡眠時間はおのずと短くなるが、それに耐えられないようなら一流の鮨屋にはなれないだろう。流通が発達した現在は、産地から直接仕入れることも可能だ。しかし、仕入れは市場に足を運ぶのが基本。毎日、全国から届く数千の魚の中から、これぞという品を競り落とす仲卸業者はプロの目利きである。その確かな目を頼ったほうが良質の品を手に入れられる。彼らのアドバイスを聞けば、魚種や産地の視野を広げることもできる。ただし、入荷した魚の中でトップクラスの魚を売ってもらうには、仲卸からの信頼を得ることが必須だ。豊洲では鮪屋1軒、鮪以外の魚を扱う小物屋1軒に絞り、あちこちの仲卸を買い回る"つまみ食い"はしない。横柄に振る舞うのもご法度。魚を分けていただくという謙虚な気持ちを常に持ち、時には売れ残りを賄いとして買う度量も必要だ。その上で肝心なのは腕を磨くこと。仲卸が認める鮨屋になることで選りすぐりの魚が回ってくる。こうした一つ一つの積み重ねこそ、仕入れの最大の極意なのである。

旬と産地

仕入れの際、常に念頭に置くのは魚の旬だ。旬とは産卵に向けて栄養を蓄えた、その魚が最も旨い時季。身が太り脂も乗った味のピークといえるだろう。産卵期は魚が沿岸に近づくため、水揚げも増える。そのため、旬は漁獲量が最も多い時季という捉え方もある。さらに、旬には「走り」と「名残り」もある。特に意識するのは走りの時季だ。味の点では早熟ながら、季節を先取りして喜んでいただく。盛りの時季より仕入れ値は高いが、それでも買ってくるのが鮨屋の心意気だ。旬を追いかけると、おのずと季節にふさわしい味になる。春には軽やかな旨みと華やかな色合いの魚が多く、食欲が落ちる夏はさっぱりした味の魚が増える。涼しい秋は脂っ気のあるものが恋しくなり、魚も脂を含んでくる。冬は寒さを凌ぐため、脂の乗った濃厚な魚に替わる。酒量が増える時季でもあり、魚もそれに見合った味になるから面白い。例外は鮪、穴子、小肌だ。これらにも旬はあるが、江戸前鮨の象徴として一年中使い続ける。最盛期に比べて多少味は落ちても、仕込みで旨くするのも大切な仕事だ。もちろん、旬の訪れは産地でも異なる。産地選びも魚の仕入れでは重要だ。名産地は良質な魚が獲れるだけでなく、漁師が獲り方に長けている、水揚げ後の処理が上手いといった多様な要素がある。輸送方法も大切だ。氷の当て方、活魚なら水槽の形状や水などで味に大きな差が出る。この点で優れているのは北海道だろう。雪の多い季節でも入荷は途切れず、輸送時間を見越した手当てがされている。もう一つ、考慮すべきなのは気候変動である。鰆は九州の佐賀と福岡が一級品だったが、現在は秋田から上質なものが入る。寒鰤は富山など日本海側が名産地とされるが、ここ数年、北海道で豊漁だ。伝統を受け継ぐことは大切だが、情報のアップデートも欠かせないのである。

〆と旨さ

「〆」は鮨屋の大切な仕事だ。〆た魚は水分がほどよく抜け、旨みも凝縮される。冷蔵庫がなかった時代には、保存の意味も大きかっただろう。中でも酢〆は江戸前の伝統的な製法の一つ。まずは塩を当て、その後、酢に浸ける。これだけで魚の味わいが変化し、〆加減によって店の個性も浮き彫りになる。とりわけ重要なのは塩の〆加減だ。塩の打ち方には淡雪とぼた雪がある。クセのない魚や水分をあまり含んでいない魚には、乾いた手で淡雪のようにさらさらと軽く塩を降らせる。より軽くするために、から煎りした塩を使うこともある。一方、クセの強い魚や水分の多い魚はぼた雪にする。このときは手を湿らせ、どさどさと厚く落とす。塩の重みも利用してアクを浮かせ、脱水を促すのである。一尾の魚の中で強弱をつけることもある。〆鯖なら脂の多い腹側はぼた雪に、背側は淡雪にする。魚を捌きながらどこにどう塩を当てるかを見極められてこそ一人前といえるだろう。実をいうと、長年、鮨は酢の料理だと思っていた。しかし、最近になって塩の料理だと強く感じるようになった。仕入れた魚の大半は塩をあて水分を調整する。シャリも塩加減が重要であり、茹で物にも塩が欠かせない。塩といかに向き合うか。それが鮨の旨さにつながるのである。魚の旨みを上げるには「熟成」という方法もある。もちろん、すべての魚が熟成に向くわけではない。鮪を筆頭に寝かせることで味わいが増す魚もあれば、すぐに使って爽やかな味わいを楽しみたい魚もある。熟成を売りにする鮨屋もあるが、熟成させた濃厚な握りばかりでは食べ飽きてしまうだろう。〆物もしかりで、大切なのは緩急のつけ方。どの魚にも満遍なく手をいれると、印象が同じになって面白みがない。どこで止めれば魚の個性を生かせるか。そのさじ加減も腕の見せどころだ。

鮨屋の流儀

鮨はお客さまの目の前で素手で握る特殊な料理だ。気持ちよく食べていただくには、清潔感がことのほか重要である。開店時に魚や酢のにおいが残るのはご法度。手の爪を整えるのはもとより、外出時には手袋で日焼けを防いでいる。重いものは持たず、車のハンドルも握らない。指先の感覚を研ぎ澄ませば、包丁から伝わる振動で脂の乗りも判断できる。余談だが、生物を扱うには手の温度は低いほうがよく、開店間際には手首から先が自然と冷たくなる。自律神経が鮨屋モードに切り替わるのだ。道具の手入れも怠らない。整った道具なら呼吸をするように仕事ができる。余計な音は立てず、包丁を置くときもそっと静かに。刃をカウンターに向けるのは包丁の清らかさを示すためである。握るときの所作も大切だ。シャリは一度で取り、足したり減らしたりはしない。手数は少ないほどよく、縁起のよい奇数に揃える。握り方は手でつまむか箸で食べるかで変えている。手と箸では持ったときに力がかかる位置が異なるからだ。一方で、カウンターの雰囲気をコントロールするのも板前の大事な役割だ。付け場に立つだけで空気を変えられるのが一流の板前だと教えられた。先代である父は「高いものと高級なものとは違う。高級なものを売るのだから、ふさわしい時間をつくれるように」とも言っていた。たとえば、一緒に来た方同士で話している間は緊張がある証拠。板前を介して会話が弾むと場に打ち解けてくる。そのきっかけをつくるのも仕事のうちだ。目配りと心配りができるようになるには経験が必要だ。「板前として脂が乗るのは55歳以降」という父の言葉が実感できる年齢にようやくなった。もちろん、食べ手にも粋に愉しむ意識が必要だ。置かれた鮨を放って話に興じるのは野暮というもの。カウンターの阿吽の呼吸から鮨屋の醍醐味は生まれるのである。

top tips for procuring fish

Securing supplies of the right fish is of sink-or-swim significance in sushi. The question of finding satisfactory seafood is a serious daily one for the sushi chef, because it is through this sourcing that flavor is largely determined. On early days I head for the market at 2 am to check out the fish before bidding commences, and discuss with the broker which I have in mind for him to win at auction. Out of the several hundred fish that come in, there might be ten at most that I actually want to buy. Thus to purchase just a few fish requires beating everyone else to market. I usually go to Toyosu, but also venture further afield to the likes of Yokohama and Kawasaki. The Yokohama market is good for fish from places like Yokosuka and Koshiba in Tokyo Bay, while Kawasaki is dominated by catches from Sagami Bay, eg Hiratsuka, Chigasaki or Enoshima. Going to the right markets, and early in the morning, is what it takes to wow customers with the best-quality fish. When it comes to procuring fish for the business, I personally would find it dull to settle for "good enough." Inevitably this means less sleep, but if you can't tolerate that, you'll never be a top sushi chef. These days improved transport links mean seafood can also be sourced straight from where it was caught or harvested, but fundamentally, buying in fish still means going to market. The wholesalers who bid for the fish they absolutely must have from among the thousands arriving every day from around Japan are skilled at spotting the finest specimens, and relying on their well-trained eye will allow you to acquire premium fish. Wholesalers can also offer advice on expanding your repertoire with new species and sources. But convincing them to sell you the best fish from those that come in requires you to gain their trust. At Toyosu I deal with just one wholesaler for tuna, and one other for the rest of my seafood, and refrain from "sampling" different businesses. Be courteous to these professionals and approach transactions from the viewpoint of them generously agreeing to share some of their haul with you. Occasionally it will be your turn to generously buy their leftovers to feed your staff. The key, in the end, is to hone your skills: become a sushi chef wholesalers accept and respect, and the finest fish will be yours. Consistently doing all the things described here is the true top tip for successfully securing the fish you need.

seasons and sources

When buying fish for the restaurant, seasonality is invariably foremost in my mind. Known as the "shun," peak season for a species is when the fish has stored nutrients ahead of spawning, and is thus at its most deliciously plump and juicily fat-suffused. Fish also move closer to the coast for spawning, increasing the chances of landing them, so the shun can also be defined as the time of year when the greatest volume of a species is caught. Within the shun there are also "hashiri" and "nagori" periods, hashiri being the very early part of the season, and nagori the tail end. As a chef I am especially conscious of the hashiri period. During hashiri, though the fish's flavor has yet to mature, customers enjoy sampling the very first of the season. Prices are higher than in peak season, but buying the fish regardless of the expense is in keeping with the sushi chef spirit. As one follows the different shun, fish seem to just naturally take on flavor befitting the time of year. In spring, many possess subtle umami and brilliant coloring, while in summer when appetites falter, cleaner flavors dominate. Cooler autumn days prompt a renewed desire for something more succulent, and fish obligingly gain more fat. Winter is the time for eating rich, oily fish to ward off the cold. It's also when people drink more alcohol, and it's interesting that fish acquire flavor to match. The exceptions to this seasonality are tuna, anago, and kohada. All do have a shun, but are served year-round as symbols of Edomae sushi. An important part of the chef's job is to find ways to ensure they taste good even when flavor declines slightly outside of their prime. Fish naturally come into season at different times in different locations, and choosing the right location to source from is another critical factor in flavor. Places renowned for a particular species not only have quality offerings, fishers there are skilled at catching the fish and handling them afterward. Transport is also important. How seafood is iced, or if sold live, the type of tank and the water, can make a huge difference to the taste. Hokkaidō scores top marks here. Shipping of fish from Japan's northern island continues uninterrupted even during heavy snow, with special measures taken in anticipation of the longer transport time. Climate change is another important consideration. The finest sawara (Spanish mackerel) once came from Saga and Fukuoka in Kyūshū, but these days top-quality specimens arrive from Akita too. Areas on the Sea of Japan side like Toyama are renowned for kan-buri (yellowtail caught at the cold time of year), but for the past few years there have been bountiful catches in Hokkaidō. Tradition is important, but so is keeping up to date with the latest developments in fish populations and movements.

curing and flavor

Curing or "shime" is a key aspect of the sushi chef's job. Curing fish removes just the right amount of moisture and concentrates umami. In pre-refrigeration days it was also vital for preservation. Vinegaring in particular is a traditional Edomae curing method that involves first salting then marinating the fish in vinegar. Even these simple steps will alter flavor, and curing to varying degrees is a sizeable point of difference among sushi restaurants. Especially important is the amount of salt curing performed. There are two ways of applying salt: awayuki (light snow) and botayuki (large, wet snowflakes). Fish with no "fishiness" and those with minimal moisture are sprinkled lightly with salt awayuki-style, using dry hands. For even lighter salting, I sometimes use dry-roasted salt. Botayuki salting is used for fish that are wetter, or stronger in flavor and aroma. For these, wet your hands and dump on plenty of salt. The weight of the salt will also bring any unsavory flavor to the surface, and help to remove moisture. Salting can also identify the strengths and weaknesses of the individual fish. For shime-saba (cured mackerel) I use botayuki salting for the fatty belly, and awayuki for the back. Being able to identify exactly where and how to salt a fish as you fillet is a mark of a true sushi professional. The fact is that for many years I thought sushi was all about vinegar, but now feel strongly that salting is the key to sushi success. I salt most of my fish to adjust its moisture level. Getting the salt seasoning right is also important for the rice, and for any simmered ingredients. How you engage with salt directly affects the taste of the sushi you make. Aging is another way of boosting fish umami, though is obviously not suitable for every species. There are fish, most prominently tuna, that benefit greatly from aging, and others that are best put to use quickly to let people savor their cleaner, more subtle palate. Some sushi restaurants make aging a sales point, but I suspect a menu consisting entirely of rich, aged nigiri would eventually pall. The same goes for cured items: variety is key. Treat every fish the same and they will all seem the same, which is interesting for neither chef nor diner. Knowing where to stop to make the best of a fish's unique features is yet another test of the sushi chef's skill.

sushi customs and conventions

Being made with bare hands in front of the customer makes sushi an unusual cuisine. A general sense of cleanliness must prevail for people to feel comfortable eating at your counter. Always make sure any lingering odors, such as of fish or vinegar, are gone by opening time. I keep my nails trimmed of course, but also wear gloves outside to avoid sunburnt hands, and refrain from lifting anything heavy or getting behind the wheel of a car. Train your fingertips to be more sensitive, and you will be able to discern the amount of fat on a fish from the vibration felt through the knife. Colder hands are better for dealing with raw foods, by the way, and I find that I naturally start to cool from the wrists down just ahead of opening time. I suppose my autonomic nervous system is switching to sushi mode. Maintaining equipment is another task that must never be neglected. Having the right gear on hand makes the sushi chef's job as natural as breathing. Avoid making excess noise, and set your knife down quietly too. Facing the blade toward the counter is designed to reassure customers that the knife is clean. Your actions when making nigiri are also important. Take the rice in one clump, never adding more or reducing. The fewer actions involved the better, and an odd number is more auspicious. How you construct the nigiri will depend on how it is to be eaten, because the force is applied in a different place depending on whether the sushi is held in a hand or chopsticks. Subtly controlling the atmosphere at the counter is another important role for the chef. I was taught that a top-class chef can alter the mood merely by taking his place behind the counter. My father, also my predecessor in the business, also noted that high-priced does not equal high-class. "We're in a luxury business, so need to make sure all the time spent at our restaurant reflects that." For example, customers who have arrived together speaking solely to each other indicates nervousness about being there, so if the chef facilitates some animated conversation, people will start to relax into the setting. Finding opportunities to do this is part of the job. This ability to read the room, so to speak, and act accordingly really only comes with experience. My father said you only hit your stride as a chef from 55 onward, and I've now finally reached the age where I truly understand that. Naturally, the diner also has to be genuinely prepared to enjoy the chef's creations: leaving the sushi placed in front of you to sit untouched while you chat does show a certain lack of sophistication. The real pleasure of being a sushi chef lies in achieving that perfect, harmonious rhythm of chef, customers and counter.

鮨種
neta (toppings)

白身 shiromi (white fish)

鮃
(hirame)

旬は10月後半から3月頃までだが、寒さが募るほど味わいを増す冬の
白身魚の代表格だ。出始めはソゲと呼ばれる1kg以下のものが多く、
師走の声を聞く頃には体も大きくなり、身の色は飴色に輝くようになる。
主な産地は青森、宮城、茨城・鹿嶋、千葉・銚子。なかでも、12月
半ばからの青森産は格別だ。身の弾力といい、奥行きのある旨みとい
い、唸るほどの旨さである。仕入れるのは、2kg前後の活け物と決め
ている。頭の付け根が厚く、目のない腹側が全体的に白く傷がないも
のを選ぶ。5枚におろし、塩をあてて水分を抜いた後、つまみにするな
ら当日中に供す。鮃特有のグリッと歯が食い込むような感触が強く、淡
く上品な味わいも堪能できる。握りには1〜2日間、寝かして旨みを上
げてから使うといい。歯応えに柔らかさが加わるため、シャリとしなや
かに融合してくれる。無垢な味わいは昆布〆にも向き、しっとりとした
舌触りのなかに洗練された旨みが開花する。さらに鮃では鰭の際にあ
る"エンガワ"にもファンは多い。コリッとした独特の歯応えと嚙むことで
広がる脂の甘みは、つまみにはもちろんのこと、握りにしても喜ばれる。

Best from late October through March, typically for a white fish hirame
acquires more taste as temperatures plummet. Initially weighing under
1kg, by close to December hirame are handsome specimens with radiant
amber flesh. Sourced mainly from Aomori, Miyagi, Kashima in Ibaraki, and
Chōshi in Chiba. Hirame caught mid-December in Aomori are especially
prized for their firm flesh, complex umami, and delectable flavor. I source
hirame live and weighing around 2kg, choosing fish solid at the base of the
head, and pale and undamaged on the underside. Cut into five pieces, salted
to remove moisture, and served the same day, with its distinctive, slightly
chewy texture and subtle, refined flavor hirame is a great match for drinks.
For nigiri the flesh is best left for a day or two to boost umami. Now more
tender, it melts almost seamlessly into the rice. Hirame's clean palate also
makes it good for kombu curing, sophisticated umami blooming amid juicy
mouthfeel. Many also consider the "edges" on hirame fins a treat, and their
distinctive crunchy texture combined with the succulent oily sweetness
released with each bite makes these a perfect snack, and a nigiri favorite too.

olive flounder

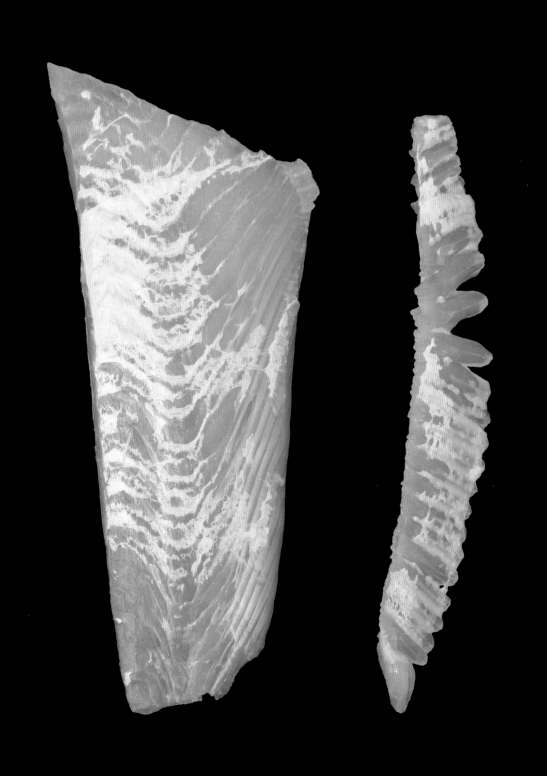

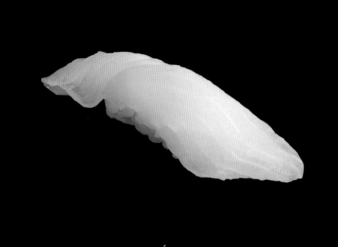

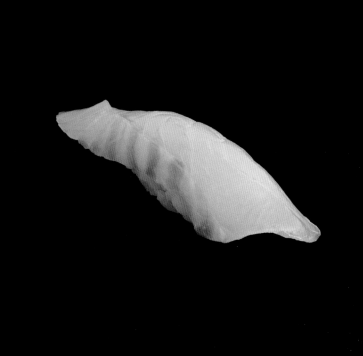

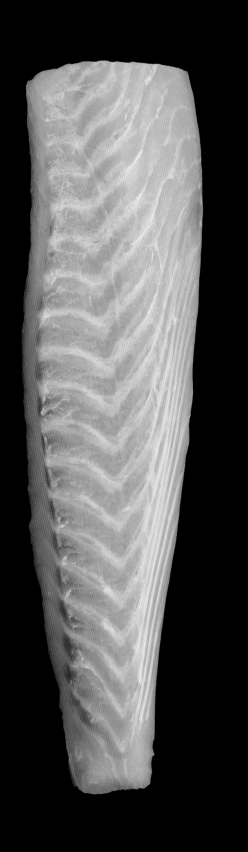

真鯛
(madai)

隅田川に架かる永代橋の桜が芽吹いたら真鯛の季節だ。築地に河岸が
あった頃には、「材木問屋が多い木場のほうから木の香りがしてきたら
鯛の時季」とも教えられた。南風が吹く時分という意味だ。旬はそこから
4月いっぱいと短い。市場には一年中並ぶが、最盛期の味は別格だ。こ
れほど極端に旬が際立つ魚は珍しいだろう。産地は兵庫・淡路、鳴門
海峡、神奈川・佐島、静岡・御前崎。荒波に揉まれて育つ鳴門鯛の旨
さはつとに知られるが、佐島の鯛も負けてない。まさに東の一級品である。
仕入れるのは2〜3kgの活け物。目の上にあるブルーのラインがくっきり
浮き出たものを選んで買い付ける。握りには昆布〆か湯引きに。湯引きの
場合、塩で水分を抜いて一晩寝かせた後、さっと熱湯にくぐらす。この
湯を純米酒に替えた贅沢な手法もある。酒に負けない旨みがあるから
こその誂えだ。真鯛の握りは見た目も味も美しい。桜色の皮が覗く白身に
は透明感があり、気品に満ちた甘みを鮮烈に解き放つ。「腐っても鯛」
という言葉を実感できる風格だ。腹に抱えた卵は薄味で煮て、頭は煮付
けたり、吸い物にしたり。桜のごとく儚い旬をそうやって味わい尽くす。

When the cherry trees of the Sumida River's Eitai Bridge are in bud,
madai are at their finest. Back when Tsukiji had a riverbank, madai were
also said to be in season when the fragrance of wood wafted from the
timber yards, that is, when the southerly winds blew. The short season
lasts only from then until the end of April. Madai are available all year
round, but a whole different taste dimension at their peak: few fish are so
obviously seasonal. Sourced from Awaji in Hyōgo, the Naruto Strait,
Sajima in Kanagawa, and Omaezaki in Shizuoka. Naruto madai, buffeted
from birth by rough seas, is legendary, but Sajima madai is just as superb.
I procure this treat from eastern Japan live at 2-3kg, choosing fish with
distinct blue lines above the eyes. For nigiri, parboil or cure with kombu.
If the former, salt to draw off moisture, leave overnight, and rinse briefly
in boiling water, or for a special touch, junmaishu sake: perfect for a fish
just as tempting. As the saying goes, "Even if it's rotten, it's still sea
bream," and with its translucent pale flesh and pink skin unleashing a blast
of intense sweetness, madai nigiri lives up to its visual and taste reputation.

red sea bream

真子鰈

(makogarei)

鱸、鯒と並ぶ夏の白身魚の代表。6月から市場に並び、8月下旬まで旬が続く。かすかに琥珀色をした身はグリッと弾力があり、プチプチと弾けるような食感がある。すっきりとした味わいは夏にふさわしく、噛み締めると上品な甘みが滲み出す。日本各地で水揚げされるが、私が店で使うのは横須賀（神奈川県）に始まり、千葉県・銚子、茨城県・鹿嶋、そして宮城県へと時季を追って北上。選ぶのは一本釣りをした活魚に限る。一本釣りは釣り針をつけたまま出荷されることが多く、手製の針が上唇にかかっていれば漁師の技量は間違いない。目利きでは鰓蓋辺りにある動脈に触れてみるのも欠かせない。力強く脈打つなら丈夫な証拠。餌をよく食べて太り、身質も引き締まっていることが想像できる。さらに、目のない裏側が純白で傷がないことも重要だ。仕込みは5枚おろしにした後、塩をあてて15〜20分おく。塩は塩水で洗い流すか、布巾で拭き取るかし、保水紙に包んで冷蔵庫で2〜3日寝かせると、縮みが取れ味も凝縮される。身と皮の間にある銀波に旨みがあるため、皮を剥ぐ際はできるだけ残すこと。ここにも板前の技量が表れる。

A white fish synonymous with summer alongside suzuki (Japanese sea bass) and kochi (flathead), makogarei appears in markets from June, and remains in season until late August. Its elastic, amber-tinged flesh pops with springy pep, while its clean flavor is ideal for summer, a refined sweetness suffusing the palate with every bite. Choose live fish caught by pole and line. These are often shipped with fishhook intact, a handmade hook in the top lip being a sign of the fisherman's skill. Don't forget to feel the arteries near the gill covers: a strong pulse is proof of robust good health, showing that the fish has probably eaten well, growing plump and firm-fleshed. The underside should be snow white and unmarked. Fillet in gomai-oroshi (five-piece) fashion, salt and set aside for 15-20 minutes. Rinse off salt with saltwater or wipe off with a cloth, wrap in moisture-absorbing paper and refrigerate for 2-3 days, to eliminate shrinkage and concentrate flavor. When skinning, leave as much of the umami-rich silvery "wave" between flesh and skin as possible; doing so successfully is another test of the sushi chef's skill.

marbled sole

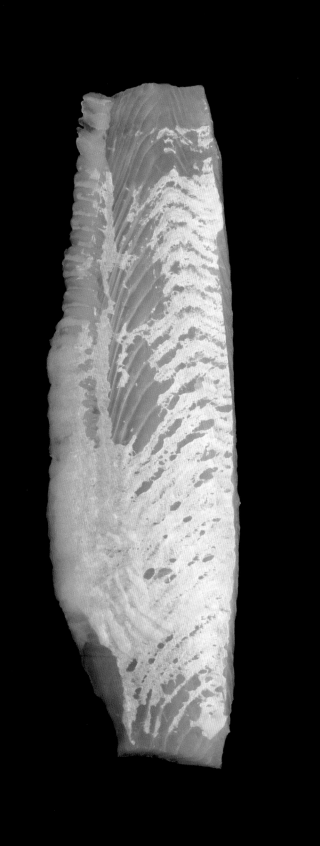

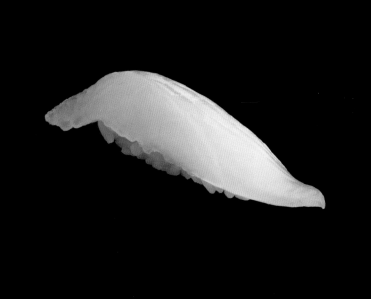

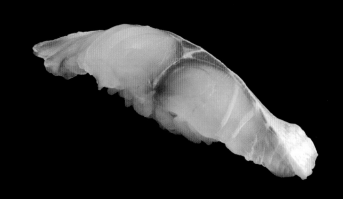

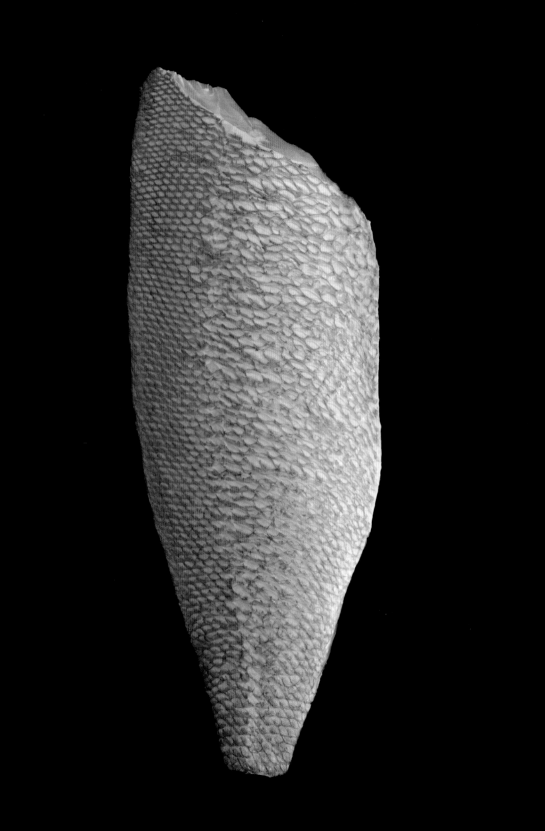

伊佐木
(isaki)

新緑が眩しい5月初旬から7月いっぱい旬が続く伊佐木だが、仕入れるのはもっぱら梅雨の間。"梅雨伊佐木"という呼び方がある通り、産卵直前のこの時季は栄養を蓄えるため最も脂が乗り、伊佐木の真骨頂を味わえる。産地は大分、佐賀、兵庫県の淡路、千葉の外房、伊豆諸島の新島と広範囲にわたるが、関東より北のものを使うことはない。市場に並ぶのは船上で締めたものがほとんど。大分・豊後水道や淡路は神経締めが主流のため、これらの産地を使うことが多い。選ぶ際は魚体がしっとり濡れたように光り、エラの付け根を鷲掴みにしたときに厚みがあるかを確認する。当然、身の厚さも重要だ。仕入れた当日は味が淡白過ぎるため、3枚に開いてから軽く塩を振って余分な水分を出す。その後、1〜2日間、熟成させて旨みを上げる工程が欠かせない。この状態で握りにすれば乳白色の身の色と血合いの紅色とのコントラストが際立ち、惚れ惚れするほど美しい。味わいは淡く上品で、すっきりとした甘みは夏場の魚ならではだろう。また、梅雨の時季は白子や真子を抱いているのも特徴だ。白子は軽く湯通ししてポン酢を添え、真子はさっと煮ればオツな酒肴になる。さまざまに楽しめるのもこの魚の魅力だ。

The isaki season runs from the dazzling new green of early May to the end of July, but isaki is best purchased at its rainy-season peak, when it has acquired ample nutritious fat ahead of spawning. Most specimens at market are dispatched on the boat, and I tend to use those from the Bungo Channel in Ōita, or Awaji, where shinkei-jime dominates. Choose fish with a moist shimmer, and grasp the base of the gills to check for flesh. Obviously there should be plenty on the body too. Isaki lacks flavor fresh, so I fillet it sanmai-oroshi style and salt to remove excess moisture, then age for 1-2 days to boost the umami: an essential step. Made into nigiri at this point, isaki is enchanting in its vivid contrast of milky-white and scarlet, blood-suffused flesh, and its mild, refined flavor and subtle sweetness make it ideal for summer dining. Rainy season isaki also carry shirako (sperm sacs) and roe: blanch shirako briefly and serve with ponzu sauce, and lightly simmer roe, for two slightly unusual but delicious accompaniments to drinks. With so many ways to enjoy it, isaki is a fish that just keeps on giving.

chicken grunt

金目鯛
(kinmedai)

鮮やかな紅色の体色と金色に輝く大きな目玉がトレードマーク。市場に並ぶ金目鯛は〝沖金目〟と〝地金目〟に大別される。沖金目は沖合で漁獲されたものを指し、体長が大きく、煮物にすると本領を発揮する。一方、地金目は最大でも1.3kgまで。餌の豊富な沿岸部で育つため、小ぶりながらも身が厚く脂の乗りも抜群だ。鮨ネタに向くのはこの地金目である。白身魚ながら脂の甘みが感じられ、旨みも豊かだ。産地は千葉県の銚子や勝浦、伊豆諸島の新島など。一年中脂が落ちないため通年使用できるが、特に11月から3月までがベストシーズンだ。選ぶ際は持ったときにずっしり重く、張りがあって胸鰭の周囲に厚みがあるかを確認する。身質に水分が多いため、塩をしっかり当てるのが鉄則だ。出し方は2通りあり、1つは皮を軽く湯引きしてそのまま握りや刺身にする方法。皮の部分の旨味としっとりとした舌触りを楽しめる。もう1つは昆布〆だ。昆布の風味を纏って、風味が一段と華やかになる。この金目鯛を鮨ネタとして使うようになったのはごく最近のこと。江戸前伝統からは外れるものの、今では引き合いの多い人気のネタになっている。

Easily recognized by its vibrant red coloring and large, glittering gold eyes, kinmedai at market are broadly divided into "oki-kinme" and "ji-kinme." The larger oki-kinme are caught out at sea and come into their own when served simmered. Ji-kinme in contrast weigh 1.3kg at the most, but inhabit the rich feeding grounds near rocky coasts, and thus though small, are sturdy with superb fat content, and better suited to sushi than their beefier cousins. A white fish that also boasts sweet, succulent fat, kinmedai are bursting with umami. Sourced from Chōshi and Katsuura in Chiba, the island of Niijima etc., kinmedai retain fat all year round so can be used any time, but are at their finest from November to March. Choose firm, heavy fish, fleshy around the pectoral fins. Salt thoroughly, as kinmedai is watery. There are two ways to serve it: lightly dowse skin in boiling water and make into sashimi or nigiri to enjoy the umami and juiciness of the skin; or kombu curing. A coating of kombu flavor raises kinmedai's own to a new level. A very recent addition to sushi repertoire, kinmedai is not part of Edomae tradition, but is now a frequently requested topping.

splendid alfonsino

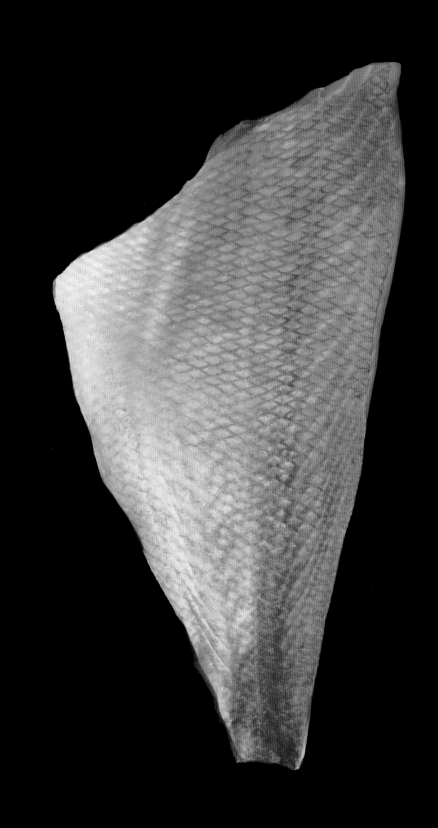

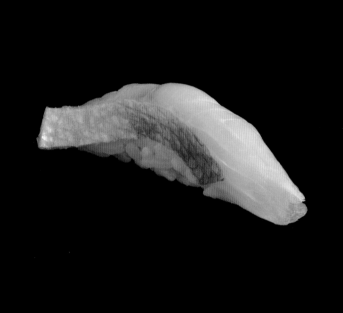

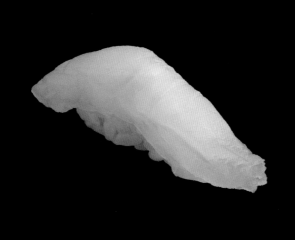

鬼笠子
(oni-kasago)

ゴツゴツしたいかつい風貌はまさしく赤鬼さながら。背びれや腹びれなどに毒針を持つのも特徴だ。イタリアンやフレンチで使われることの多い鬼笠子は、江戸前の鮨ネタとしては異色の存在ではあるものの、握りにして味が引き立つ白身魚である。旬は6月から8月の夏。ただし、海底の岩礁などに棲み付いた根付き魚のため、旬を外れても極端に味に差が出ることはない。使い勝手がよい反面、漁獲量が少ないことから市場では高級魚になっている。買うのは房総半島の富津や布良、平砂浦の南側で獲れたものが多い。釣り好き垂涎の釣果でもあり、釣り番組では2kg超えの大物を見かけるが、市場に出回るのは小型が主流。そのなかからできるだけ大きく、ずんぐり太ったものを見繕う。毒針に注意しながら捌いた後は寝かせずに、仕入れたその日から使うことがほとんどだ。カウンターで感嘆の声が挙がるのは、いかつい見た目とは裏腹の可憐な味わいゆえである。透き通った身肉はプリッとほどよい弾力があり、噛みしめると軽やかで透明感のある甘みが迸る。その旨さは伊勢海老に匹敵すると評されるほど。この魚を専門に狙う釣り人の気持ちがわかるはずだ。

Craggy, fearsome features give the oni-kasago its devilish (*oni*) reputation, reinforced by the poisonous spines on its fins. Used frequently in Italian and French cuisine, this outré member of the Edomae sushi pantheon is a white fish whose flavor is best showcased as nigiri. Oni-kasago peaks in the summer months from June to August, but due to its non-migratory bottom-dwelling reef habits, remains largely consistent in flavor year-round. Its versatility combined with the small size of the catch makes it undoubtedly an upmarket fish option. A prized amateur catch as well, specimens over 2kg are seen on TV fishing programs, but the commercial market is dominated by smaller fish. The trick is to select the biggest, sturdiest specimens. I usually use oni-kasago the same day, after careful filleting to avoid the spines. The exclamations of delight from customers are due to the exquisite flavor that belies this fish's forbidding appearance, the translucent flesh offering just the right amount of chewiness, each bite suffused with a light, limpid sweetness said to rival that of spiny lobster. It's no wonder so many fishers exclusively pursue this piscine diamond in the rough.

scorpion fish

魴鮄
(hōbō)

浮き袋から「ボォ、ボォ」と鳴き声のような音を出すのが名前の由来と言われている。全身が赤味を帯び、背中に薄い群青色のまだら模様が浮かぶ。アゲハ蝶に似た大きく色鮮やかな胸鰭を持ち、足のような細長い鰭を使って海底を歩行するなどなかなかユニークな魚である。旬は11月から2月の冬場。千葉・銚子産が最高と言われている。背中の群青色がツヤツヤと美しく、目が澄んでしっかり張りがあるものほど新鮮だ。角張った大きな頭に反して胴はスリムなため、歩留まりがよいとは言えない。前のめりで使いたい魚ではないが、市場には時折、そそられるほどよい品が大量に入荷することがあり、そのときは率先して仕入れている。仕込みは軽く塩をあてて水分を抜き、寝かせるのは長くても一晩。もともとさほど水っぽさはなく、また長く置くと血合いの色が変わり、握りにしたときの美しさが損なわれるのも早めに使う理由だ。なめらかな白身はほどよい歯応えがあり、とろっとした甘みを兼ね備えている。肝も茹でると旨く、刺身に添えるなどつまみに格好だ。ちなみに、江戸時代には「君魚」と呼ばれ、殿様が食べる上等な魚だったそうである。

Named for the "*bo, bo*" grunting sound from its swim bladder, the hōbō is red with pale ultramarine mottling. Large pectoral fins as vibrantly colored as the wings of a swallowtail, and long, thin leg-like fins used to perambulate along the sea floor, make this one unique fish. Tastiest in winter, from November to February, with the finest sourced from Chōshi in Chiba. The freshest hōbō have glossy, attractive back spots, clear eyes, and firm flesh. With a slim torso in contrast to its large angular head, hōbō is a low-yield species best used perhaps not as a first choice for sushi, but on the odd occasion that temptingly high-quality specimens land in quantity. Lightly salting to draw off moisture, and leaving overnight at longest, I use hōbō promptly because it is not very watery to start with, and if left too long the dark parts of its flesh will change color, reducing its visual appeal as nigiri. The smooth white flesh is slightly firm to the bite, and meltingly sweet. The poached liver is also delicious, and a perfect snack, perhaps with sashimi. In the Edo period hōbō was Japan's "fish of kings," its consumption largely a privilege of the ruling elite.

red gurnard

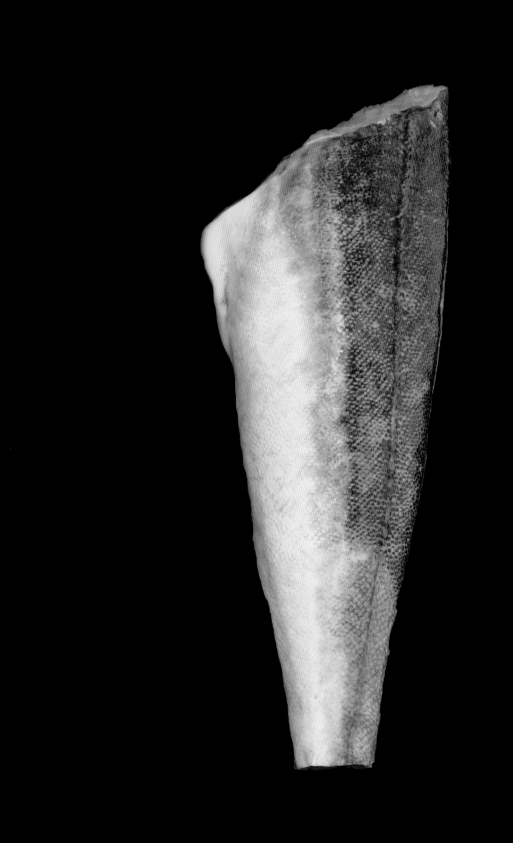

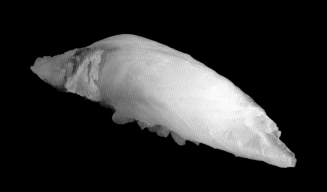

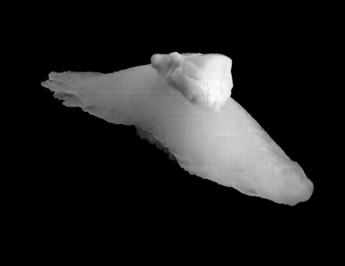

皮剥
(kawahagi)

秋が深まる10月から年明け1月頃までを旬とする皮剥は、肝あっての魚である。淡白で上品な身に対して、肝はねっとりとして濃厚。両者を合わせることで、バランスの取れた無二の味が生まれる。そのため、何より肝心なのは肝の鮮度である。産地は全国に広がるが、東京の鮨屋の間では流通に時間がかからない東京湾産が最上とされる。湾内で水揚げが多いのは、羽田、神奈川県の横須賀や佐島、千葉県金谷など。市場には活け締めも並ぶが、仕入れるのは活け物と決めている。そのなかでもお腹がこんもりしたものは、たっぷりの肝を期待できる。仕込みも重要だ。淡白な身は塩をあてて余分な水分を抜く作業が不可欠。シコッとした歯応えが生まれ、旨味も凝縮される。一方、肝は20〜40分ほど氷水つけて血を固まらせるのが最初の工程。ピンセットで血管を1本ずつ剥ぐように取り除いた後、軽く酒に浸せばクセが抜けて澄んだ旨みが楽しめる。握りの場合は煮切り醤油をひいた上に叩いた肝を載せ、つまみは厚めに切りつけた身とともに肝を盛り付け醤油を添える。白身と肝が口の中で一つになったとき、河豚にひけを取らない極上の味わいが生まれる。

Kawahagi, in season from October to about January, is prized for its sticky, intensely flavorful liver, which contrasts with its subtle, delicate flesh. Together they achieve a unique and delectable balance. The freshness of the liver is therefore paramount. Kawahagi is caught all over Japan, but among Tokyo chefs that from Tokyo Bay, such as Haneda, Yokosuka and Sajima in Kanagawa, and Kanaya in Chiba, is deemed best, due to proximity. Markets offer an ikejime option, but I always buy live specimens, choosing those with nice rounded bellies swollen with liver. Prepping is key: salting the mild flesh to draw off excess moisture is critical, giving a firmer bite, and more concentrated umami. Prepare the liver meanwhile by first placing in iced water for 20-40 minutes so that the blood coagulates. After peeling away the blood vessels individually with tweezers, steep briefly in sake to remove any overtly "raw" taste and enjoy a pure umami hit. For nigiri, brush on nikiri sauce then place pounded liver on top. For a snack, arrange liver with thick slices of the fish's flesh and serve with shōyu. The combo of white flesh and liver is a taste sensation to rival fugu.

thread-sail filefish

鰤
(kamasu)

秋刀魚に似た細長い姿が特徴。種類は赤鰤と大和鰤に大別される。赤鰤は背中が薄茶色、腹側は乳白色と2色に分かれて鱗も多い。生食にも向き、鮨ネタになるのはこの赤鰤である。対して、大和鰤は背の色がやや青味がかり腹の色と混じる。身質が水っぽく、干物にするのがもっぱらだ。ちなみに、両者は鰭の位置も異なり、見分けるのは容易だ。値段の高さでも赤鰤に軍配が上る。産地は小田原の早川、千葉・富津が中心。旬は3月〜4月と10月〜12月の年2回ある。春は産卵前で脂が乗り、冬は産卵から体が戻って脂を蓄える時季。どちらも遜色ない旨さだ。仕入れるものは体長50cm前後、体高10cmほどの大型だ。餌ではなく身肉によって、腹がはち切れんばかりに張っているものがよい。一般的にはさっぱりしたイメージがあるが、旬は脂もたっぷり。半日から1日寝かすと脂の甘みが一段持ち上がり、とろっと柔らかな口当たりが楽しめる。元来、江戸前の鮨ネタにはなく、店で使い始めたのはレストランで鰤のカルパッチョを食べたのがきっかけだった。思えば、四国や九州など各地の郷土料理には鰤の姿寿司がある。シャリと相性がよいのは当然だ。

Kamasu are broadly divided into two species: red and Yamato, both with distinctive sleek saury-like bodies. The red kamasu has a light brown back and milky-white belly, is heavily scaled, and being the species most suitable for eating raw, is used in sushi. In contrast, the back of the Yamato kamasu has a blue tinge that blends into its underside, and more watery flesh, making it ideal for drying. Different positioning of the fins also makes it easy to distinguish between the two. There are two seasons: March-April and October-December. In spring, the fish acquire fat before spawning, and in winter, again as their bodies recover. Kamasu from both seasons are equally delicious. Sushi kamasu are large, around 50cm long, and 10cm high. Kamasu are generally seen as having a clean flavor, but in season also have plenty of fat. Curing for a half to a whole day raises the sweetness of this fat a notch, for a melt-in-the-mouth, tender taste experience. Kamasu is not originally an Edomae species; I first used it in sushi after eating it as carpaccio in a restaurant. Kamasu as sugata sushi is actually found in many regional cuisines, and thus is an obvious match for sushi rice.

barracuda

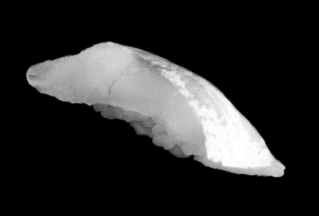

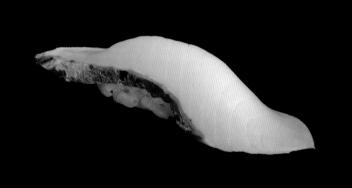

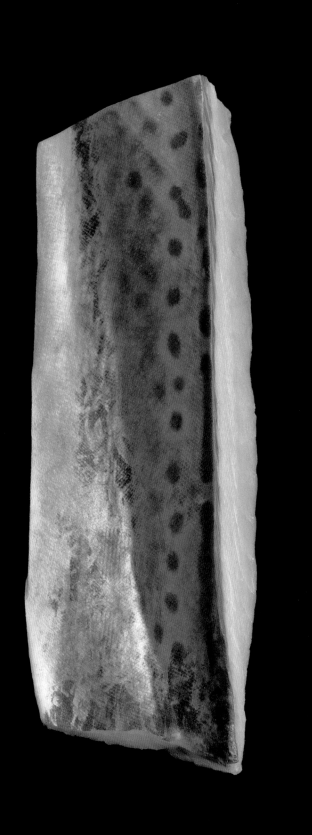

鰆
(sawara)

成長するに従い名前を変える出世魚。関東では50㎝くらいまでを「サ
ゴシ（サコチ）」と呼び、それ以上を鰆とすることが多い。春の文字が
つく魚だが、脂が乗って旨いのは11月から2月ぐらいまで。「寒鰆」と
称すこともある。産地は千葉・房州、静岡・舞阪、九州全域。特に房
州は脂の乗りがよく、身がしっかりとした良品が多い。仕入れるのは体
長1mに及ぶ大物だ。体色が薄い青色よりも、少し黒が混じった青
光りするものがよい。身割れしやすい魚のため、仕込みではほかの魚
以上に丁寧に扱う必要がある。三枚におろした後、片身を3等分して
から身に軽く塩をふって余分な水分を抜く。これに串を打ち、皮目を藁
で炙って握りや刺身にするのが常だ。こうすると皮もおいしく食べられ、
皮の下の脂も余すことなく味わえる。繊細な風味を損ねないよう、炙
り加減はごく軽く。藁の香りがつかない程度に抑えることがポイントであ
る。柔らかい身はふわりとなめらかで、甘みも軽く心地よい。とろっとし
た脂の甘みが楽しめるのは、まさに冬の鰆ならではと言える。癖がない
ので好みに左右されず、刺身の盛り合わせの1品に加えても喜ばれる。

Known in Kantō as "sagoshi" or "sakochi" up to about 50cm, and usually
"sawara" (or "kan [cold] sawara") thereafter. The kanji for sawara
contains that for spring, but this mackerel is actually at its fat-smothered
succulent best between November and February. I purchase large
specimens up to a meter in length, preferably a shimmery blue mixed
with a hint of black, rather than uniformly light blue. Sawara is fragile
and needs more delicate handling than many other fish. Fillet sanmai-
oroshi style and cut each piece into three equal chunks, salt lightly, and
wipe off excess moisture. I usually then thread the chunks on skewers,
grill the skin side on straw, and serve as nigiri or sashimi, allowing the
skin to be savored as well, plus every last bit of fat underneath. Very
gentle grilling maintains the delicate flavor, the trick being to keep the
flame down to a level that stops the fish smelling of straw. The tender
flesh is soft and smooth, the sweetness pleasantly subtle. Mouthwatering
oily succulence is what distinguishes winter sawara, its mildness giving it
widespread appeal and making it a great addition to any sashimi platter.

Spanish mackerel

真鯒
(magochi)

上から押し潰したような平たい体と大きな鰭を持ち、海底の砂地を這うように暮らすのが真鯒である。旬は6月から8月。梅雨が明けてからが勝負の魚だ。「照り鯒」とも呼ばれるように、日照りが続くと味わいが増す。真子鰈や平鱸と並ぶ夏の白身の真打である。東京湾、茨城・福島の常磐、九州などの産地のものが市場に並ぶが、高級とされるのは千葉・富津だ。店では主にこの産地の活け物を仕入れている。触ったときに体を覆うぬめりが強く、胴回りが太いほどよい。直径15cmに達すればかなりの上物だ。魴鮄と同様、頭がドンと大きく尻尾に向けてスーッと細くなる体形から歩留まりは芳しくない。身の量を考えると割高の魚だ。さらに厄介なのは小骨が多くて抜きにくいことだ。活け物の場合、おろしたては死後硬直が強いため、なおのこと一筋縄ではいかない。身を傷めないよう丁寧に根気よく作業するのはひと苦労だ。それでも仕入れたくなるのは、やはり旨いからである。1日寝かせてから握ると、シコシコとした歯触りとともにかすかな甘みがじわりと浮き上がる。父は「潔いほど淡白な味」と言っていたが、それだけ上品で素晴らしい魚ということである。

Magochi, with their squashed bodies and large fins, spend their lives crawling along sandy seabeds, are in season from June to August, and best eaten after the rainy season. They are also known as "terigochi" due to acquiring flavor with sustained sunny weather (*teri*). A star performer in the summer white fish stakes alongside makogarei (marbled flounder) and hirasuzuki (blackfin seabass), like gurnard the magochi's large head and narrowing toward the tail makes it not the best fish in flesh-for-cash terms. Another downside is the number of tiny, tenacious bones. The rigor mortis that sets in quickly in live fish after filleting makes preparation even less straightforward. Working carefully and patiently in a way that does not damage the flesh is tricky. Yet despite all this, the magochi's flavor makes it sought-after by sushi chefs, who choose the sturdiest, slimiest specimens. Any over 15cm across are especially top quality. Aging for a day before making into nigiri draws out a faint hint of sweetness to accompany the fish's chewy texture. My father described the taste of magochi as "so plain as to be pure," which sums up the refined nature of this splendid fish.

flathead

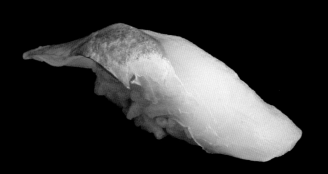

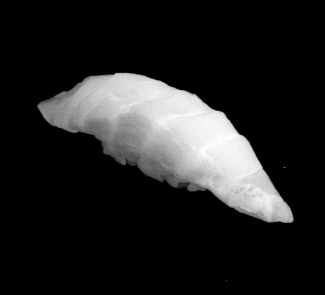

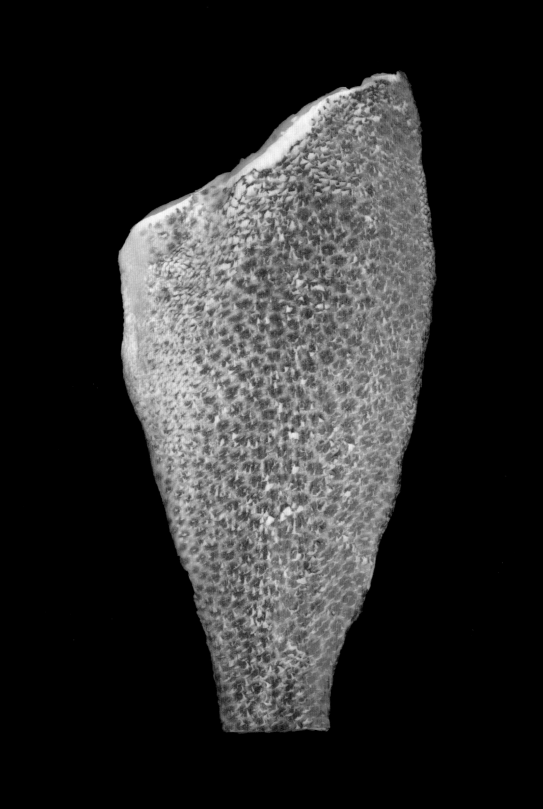

大紋羽太

(ōmonhata)

関東では雉羽太とも呼ばれ、口先から尾鰭まで全身に広がる細かい褐色の斑紋が特徴。1年を通じて味は落ちにくいが、旬は7月から10月頃とされ、店でも夏に出すことが多い。産地は長崎、鹿児島、和歌山が有名で、昨今は温暖化により東京湾や外房でもよく獲れる。好んで仕入れるのは釣り物の長崎産だ。近種の真羽太には10kgを超える大物もあるが、大紋羽太は大きくても6kg前後。使いやすく味ものった2〜3kgを仕入れている。他の魚と同様、目が澄んでエラの内側の赤味が鮮やかなことに加え、斑紋がくっきり濃いほど鮮度がよい。仕込みで気をつけるのは包丁の入れ方だ。身が割れやすいため、普段以上に慎重に行なう必要がある。三枚におろしたら表面に軽く塩を打ち、15分ほど置いた後、塩を拭き取って冷蔵庫で寝かせる。使うのは翌日以降。握りにすると淡い桜色の血合いが美しく、口当たりはもちっとして柔らかい。甘みや旨みもほどよく、上質な白身魚といえるだろう。さらに、この魚は劣化の速度も遅いため、比較的長く使い続けられる点もありがたい。海が荒れ白身魚の仕入れに困ったとき、市場で見つけると助けられた気持ちになる。

Also known in Kantō as kijihata, ōmonhata is distinguished by its head-to-tail covering of dainty brown spots. Though fairly consistent in flavor all year, it is deemed in season from July to around October, and I too tend to serve it more in summer. Its close relation the mahata (sevenband grouper) includes large fish over 10kg, but ōmonhata weigh around 6kg at most. I buy the flavorful, versatile specimens weighing 2-3kg, preferably pole-and-line caught from Nagasaki. In addition to the clear eyes and red under gills that generally signify freshness, look for clear, dark spots. Preparation requires special care with cutting, as ōmonhata flesh disintegrates more easily than most. Fillet sanmai-oroshi style, salt lightly and leave for 15 minutes, then wipe off salt and refrigerate. Use from the following day onward. In nigiri, the pale pink chiai flesh of this premium white fish with the perfect sweetness and umami is lovely to behold, and soft and springy to the bite. Ōmonhata also keeps exceptionally well, allowing it to be used for a relatively long time. When seas are rough and white fish hard to source, this is one species always a boon to find at market.

areolate grouper

九絵
(kue)

10月から2月までの寒い時季にたっぷり脂を蓄える羽太の仲間の大型魚である。大きいものは体長1m超、重さ50kg以上に及ぶ。ただし、大き過ぎると筋の入り方が強く、鍋物にはよいが生食には向かないため、2～5kgのものを選ぶようにしている。最近は養殖も盛んだが、買うのは天然物。長崎や高知が名産地として知られ、長崎の隠岐や男女群島の品を選ぶことが多い。市場に並ぶのは大半が活け〆だが、活魚があればそれを仕入れる。活魚は〆方が重要だ。まず頭と尻尾に包丁を入れ、背骨の下にある動脈の血を抜く。同時に、動脈の上にある神経をきれいに取り除くことも肝心だ。こうすると身に血が飛んだり、身が焼けて酸っぱくなることもない。丸ごと寝かせる場合は内臓を出して塩水で洗ってから、さらしの布を丸めて入れて炊飯紙などで包んで冷蔵庫へ。毎日さらしを交換しながら1週間ほど寝かせてから使いだす。熟成させた身は澄んだ琥珀色に色づき、血合いの淡い色との調和も美しい。口にすればもっちり柔らかく、脂を含んだ旨みがふわりと浮き上がる。九州では"魚の王様"と珍重されているが、それに違わぬ堂々たる味わいだ。

A relative of the hata that grows fat and sleek in the cold months between October and February, the kue is a big boy on the sushi block, the largest being more than a meter long and weighing in at over 50kg. Too big though brings a certain stringiness; good for nabe dishes, but not for eating raw, so I choose fish 2-5kg in size. Farmed kue account for a good slice of the market these days, but I only buy wild. Most found at markets have been dispatched by ikejime, but I choose any live specimens available. The technique used to kill the fish is important: insert knife in head and tail to drain blood from the artery under the backbone. At the same time, neatly remove the nerve above the artery. This will prevent blood spattering on the flesh, or the flesh burning and turning sour. To age whole, gut, rinse with saltwater, roll up a bleached cotton cloth and insert in the cavity, wrap in condensation-absorbing paper and refrigerate. Age for a week or so, changing cloth daily, before starting to use. The flesh will turn a clear amber, complementing the pale chiai. Soft and springy, kue offers an irresistible hit of fat-suffused umami in every bite.

longtooth grouper

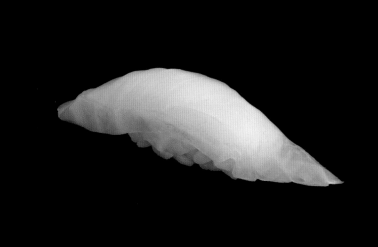

平鱸
(hirasuzuki)

夏の白身御三家の一角を担うのが鱸。江戸前伝統の鱸は丸鱸という種類で、川魚に似た独特の香りが強い。それゆえ好みが分かれ、クセを和らげるよう洗いにするなどひと手間が必要だ。一方、平鱸は独特のクセがなく、澄んだ味わいが特徴。脂の乗りもよいため、最近はもっぱらこちらを仕入れている。両者は生息域が異なり、丸鱸が棲むのは湾内など穏やかな海域。対して、平鱸は荒磯や外洋を好み、丸鱸のように川に遡上する習性もない。そうしたことが味に影響しているのだろう。旬は明確でなく、漁獲量も少なめだ。警戒心が強いため、鳥に狙われる危険性のない白波が立つときに餌を追って姿を現す。海が荒れていたほうがよく獲れるという漁師泣かせの習性がある。産地は東京湾よりも南側が多く、仕入れるのは房州が中心。活け締めが圧倒的で、触って身がしっかりし、目が澄んで鰓の内側の赤い部分が鮮やかなものを選ぶ。塩をあて水分をほどよく抜いた後に1日寝かせるが、翌日でも獲れたてと同じコリコリとした噛み応えが続くのが面白い。脂が乗っていてもすっきりとして甘みも爽やか。旬は定かでないものの夏に出したい1貫だ。

Seabass is one of Japan's "big three" summer white fish. The traditional Edomae bass was marusuzuki, which has a distinctive, potentially off-putting aroma akin to that of a river fish, reduced by rinsing. Hirasuzuki on the other hand has a mild, clean, summer-friendly palate, plus plenty of fat, so has become my go-to seabass. Marusuzuki live in calm inshore waters, and hirasuzuki rocky coasts or the open sea. Hirasuzuki do not swim up rivers like their similar-but-different cousins either, which doubtless also influences their taste. Catches are small, and season indeterminate. Cautious fish, hirasuzuki show themselves chasing feed when there are whitecaps on the water, and thus no danger from birds. Sadly for fishers, they are easier to catch in rough seas. Most hirasuzuki come from Tokyo Bay south, and I source mine primarily from Bōshū. The majority of hirasuzuki are dispatched by ikejime, and I choose those firm to the touch, clear-eyed, and bright red under the gills. Salted to properly remove moisture and aged for a day, interestingly their flesh retains the same freshly-caught springy texture. Hirasuzuki has a fresh, non-cloying sweetness even when fatty.

blackfin seabass

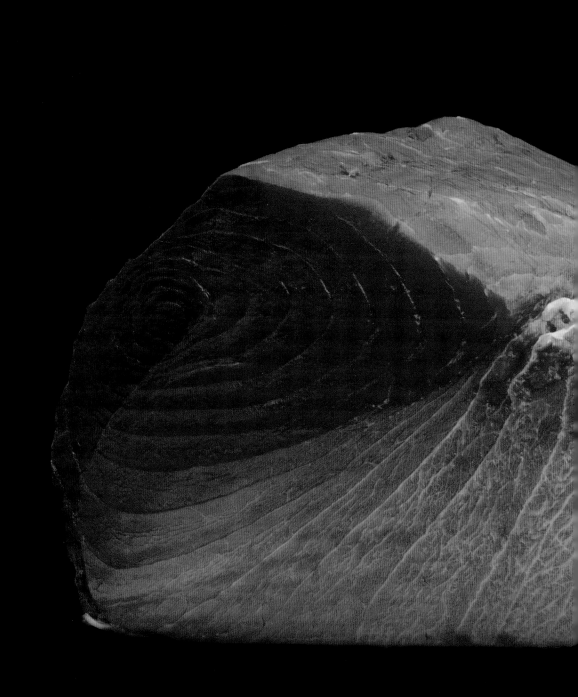

赤身 akami (red-flesh fish)

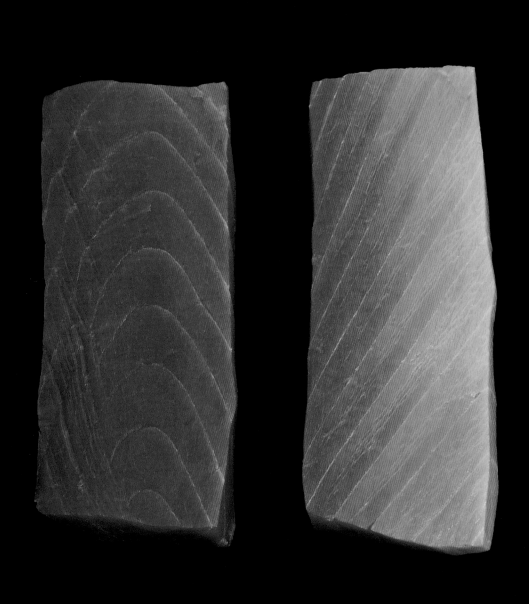

鮪
(maguro)

紛うことなき鮨の花形である。鮪なくして江戸前鮨は成り立たず、小肌や穴子同様、一年通して切らすことはない。仕入れるのは鮪の王様、黒鮪だ。回遊魚のため産地は季節で替わり、冬なら北海道の噴火湾や松前、青森の大間や尻労。春にはやや南下した岩手の宮古、夏にはさらに南に下った和歌山・勝浦、山口・萩、宮崎・油津、秋になる頃には長崎・対馬、新潟・佐渡へ。旬としては脂をたっぷり蓄えた冬になるが、夏のさっぱりした味わいにも魅力がある。市場には200kg超の大物も並ぶが、好んで仕入れるのは小ぶりの90kgサイズだ。ずっしりとした味わいのなかに軽やかさを備え、飽きず食べられる。漁法を選ぶなら釣り物、巻網、定置網のいずれか。漁師の腕も重要だ。鮪は泳ぎを止めると一気に体温が上がって火傷を起こす。獲り方や船に上げるタイミングがことさら重要になるのだ。市場には鮪専門の仲卸があり、すべてを熟知した上でこれぞという鮪を競り落とす。それを背と腹に分け、さらに頭側からカミ、ナカ、シモに分割した12の部位を販売する。仕入れるのは、トロと中トロに赤身も取れる"腹カミ"と、赤身が多く中トロも含む"背のナカ"。流通時に上側になる"上身"であることも譲れない。下身は重さがかかり、血が回って身崩れしやすいからだ。仕入れた塊は専用の紙に包んで寝かせ、落ち着いてきたら柵に分けてさらに熟成させる。最低でも4〜5日、長ければ数週間寝かせることもある。柵の周りに"ガク"と呼ばれる黒い縁取りが出た時がピークだ。身がしっとりとして、鮪ならではの香りが生まれる。切り付けは繊維がほぐれるよう重い包丁でゆっくりと行い、少し空気に触れさせておくと香りが立ちやすい。味わいは三者三様だ。赤身は血潮がもたらす香りが鼻に抜け、爽やかな酸味が持ち味。鉄火巻きの色気のある美しさにも惚れ惚れする。大トロは蛇腹の筋さえすーっと妖艶に溶けていく。もう少し噛み応えがあり、爽やかな甘みも感じる"かのこ"も人気の部位だ。トロの甘みと赤身の酸味を併せ持つ中トロは、一見客の好みを掴むのにも向く。「鮪は無理をしても高いものを買え」とは父の言葉だが、まさしく華やかな1貫には鮨職人の誇りと意地が詰まっている。

Without maguro, sushi's indisputable star turn, there is no Edomae, so I make sure to have a constant supply of Pacific bluefin, the king of tuna. At its fatty finest in winter, tuna's clean summer taste is another delight. Markets display behemoths of 200kg or more, but I prefer their more compact, 90kg cousins, boasting a rich yet lighter flavor that never palls. Choose fish caught by hook and line, purse seine net, or set net. Once tuna stop swimming their body temperature rises quickly, causing burning, which makes the fishing method and timing of landing on the boat critical. At market are wholesalers who specialize in tuna, first examining the fish available, then picking one and winning it at auction. Next the tuna is divided into back and belly, then top, middle and bottom, making a total of twelve parts for sale. I buy "top belly," which has toro and chūtoro, and also akami (red meat), and "middle back" which is mainly akami, with some chūtoro. I also insist on "uwami" flesh from the side of the fish kept upward throughout transport and sale, because the underside ends up taking the weight of the fish and has more blood draining into the flesh, making it more fragile. I wrap the block of tuna in paper kept for that purpose, rest it, and when it has settled, cut into saku blocks. The previous page shows, from left, akami, chūtoro, ōtoro, and the "sunazuri" area on the very base of the belly, also known as the "snake belly." From here the tuna is aged for at least 4-5 days, up to a few weeks, and peaks when a black border known as the "gaku" (frame) appears around the edges of the block. The flesh will be moist and exude that distinctively tuna tang. Cut slowly with a heavy knife to break up the fibers, exposing slightly to air to encourage the scent. The color will also be vibrant in nigiri. On the next page, on the left is akami, on the right sunazuri. The akami has a bloody aroma and bracing tartness, while the fat-suffused sunazuri dissolves bewitchingly in the mouth, right down to the sinews. Chūtoro, which combines the sweetness of toro and acidity of akami, is also good for determining the preferences of new customers. My father always said buy the most expensive tuna you can, and a splendid tuna nigiri does indeed contain all the pride and honor of the chef.

tuna

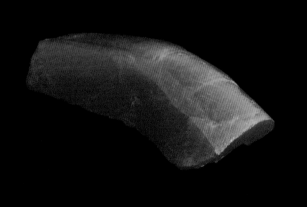

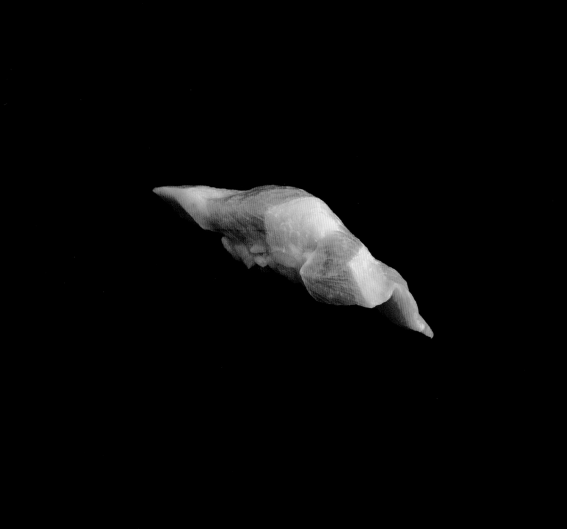

鰹
(katsuo)

旬は年に2回。最初の旬が3月から5月の初鰹だ。鹿児島で獲れ始め、メインは和歌山・勝浦。赤身魚特有の香りと酸味を持つが軽く爽やかで春にふさわしい。一方、8月中旬から10月に獲れる戻り鰹は脂が乗り、ねっとりとした身質と旨みの深さが特徴だ。産地は宮城県気仙沼が頂点だろう。鰹の漁法では一本釣りが有名だが、買うのは曳釣り限定だ。一本釣りは釣った鰹を威勢よく船内に飛ばすため、衝撃で血生臭くなりやすいからだ。そのなかで選ぶのは鰓の内側が真紅で、体表がツヤツヤと青光りしているもの。尾の付け根がザラザラしていれば鮮度がよい証拠だ。ただし、慎重に選んでも30匹に1匹の割合で食べられないほど身の硬い"ゴリ"が混じるから厄介である。仕入れた鰹は5枚におろし血合いを取り除いた後、塩をあてて水分を抜く。使うのは当日中。劣化が早いため、鮮度を優先させるのが鉄則だ。背中側は皮を引いて刺身に、腹側は皮目を藁で強めに炙ってから握る。藁の香りに負けない力強さが鰹の持ち味だ。父の世代までの鮨屋は初鰹しか使わなかったと聞く。旨さでは戻り鰹だが、感動があるのは初物。江戸前の特有の美学である。

Katsuo peaks twice a year, the hatsugatsuo (first bonito) arriving from March to May. Pole-and-line is the best-known technique for catching katsuo, but I only buy fish caught by trawling, because pole-and-line katsuo are hauled onto the boat with some force, and can be bloodied by the impact. Choose specimens bright red under the gills, with a smooth, glistening blue body. Roughness at the base of the tail is proof of freshness. Yet no matter how carefully you choose, one in 30 katsuo will unfortunately be what is known as a "gori," with tough, inedible flesh. Cut and fillet the katsuo into five pieces and remove the blood-suffused parts (chiai), then salt to draw off moisture. Use the same day. Katsuo deteriorates quickly, so freshness is all. Skin the back and use for sashimi, fire-sear the belly on straw a for nigiri. Katsuo's natural flavor is every bit as powerful as the straw's aroma. Word has it that sushi chefs up to my father's time only used hatsugatsuo. The later "modori" (returning) katsuo of August to October taste better, but people always get excited by the first of the season: part of that uniquely Edomae aesthetic.

bonito

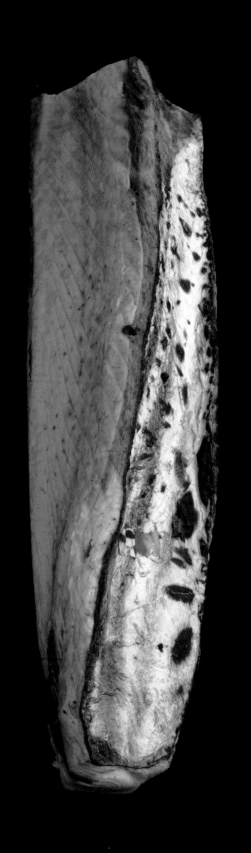

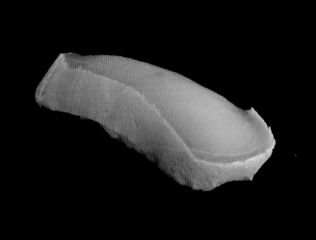

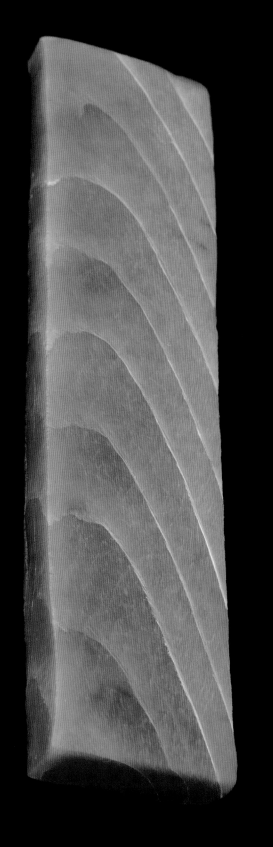

真梶木
(makajiki)

上顎から伸びた尖った口先が特徴的な大型の回遊魚。名前や姿形が似ているため女梶木と混同されやすいが、鮨にして旨いのは真梶木である。赤身の魚ながら色味は淡く舌触りはなめらか。クセがないのですっと軽快に食べられる。脂っこいものが好まれなかった時代には、率先してこれを握る鮨屋が多かったようだ。旬は冬。三陸から千葉・勝浦の広範囲でよく獲れる。買うのは、突きん棒漁で獲れたものと決めている。これは船上から銛を投げて魚を射止める昔ながらの漁法だ。餌を追って海面近くに上ってきた勇猛果敢で食欲旺盛な真梶木を狙うため、ふっくら肥えて脂の乗りもよいことが多い。さらに、突きん棒の漁師は総じて内臓を処理するスピードが速く、納得のいく品が仕入れやすい。市場では鮪と同じく腹と背に分け部位で売られるが、買うのは決まって赤身が多い"背のナカ"。寝かせてから柵取りした後、さっと湯引きしてヅケにするのがもっぱらだ。漬け時間はおおよそ1時間。こうすると淡白過ぎるところを上手く補え、味わいも深くなる。柵でヅケにするため、ほんのり優しい紅色はそのまま。握りにすると端正な美しさが目を引く。

This large migratory fish distinguished by the pointed snout extending from its upper jaw is often confused with swordfish (mekajiki) due to their similarity, but makajiki makes better sushi. Though a red-fleshed species, makajiki is pale and smooth on the palate, making mild, pleasant eating. A lot of sushi restaurants seem to have proactively offered it when oilier fish were out of fashion. At its prime in winter. I always buy makajiki caught using the old-fashioned harpoon method. This targets the bolder, hungrier fish that come to the surface to feed, which tend to be plumper with more fat. Harpoon fishers are also reliably quick at gutting, making it easy to source satisfactory specimens. The fish are separated into back and belly for sale like tuna, and I always buy the "center back," which is mainly red meat. Generally after aging the fish and cutting into slabs, I rinse briefly in boiling water and marinate for an hour or so. This compensates for any parts lacking in taste, and intensifies the overall flavor. Because it is marinated in slabs, a gentle hint of red remains. Tidily attractive, makajiki nigiri makes an eye-catching treat.

striped marlin

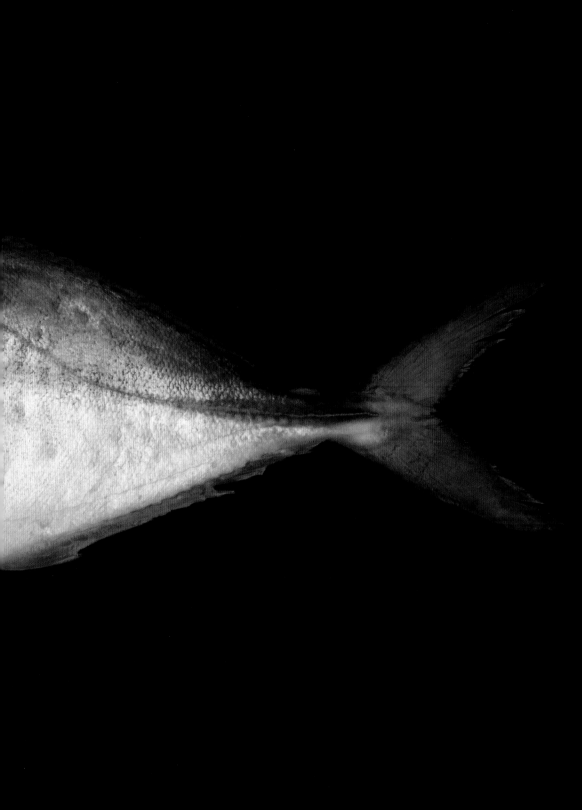

青物 aomono (blue fish)

嶋鯵
(shima-aji)

縦の縞模様がトレードマークの大型の鯵。6月から8月が最盛期で、太平洋側での水揚げが多い。好んで買うのは伊豆諸島の新島産。小ぶりながら天然物が手に入る。養殖が盛んな昨今、養殖場から逃げ出した"天然風"の嶋鯵が増えているが、純粋な天然物の旨さは段違いだ。特に上品な甘みは天然物にしかない。身も引き締まり、コリッとした心地よい弾力が楽しめる。同じ青物の魚には柔らかく脂たっぷりの鰤と、さっぱりとしてコリコリした歯応えが身上の平政があるが、嶋鯵の味わいはちょうどその中間といったところだ。市場に出回る天然物はほとんどが活け締め。体に張りがあり、皮目が瑞々しく、黒目が鮮やかなものを選ぶ。筋肉の張りにクセがないのでおろしやすく、皮を引くときは身との間にある銀波を残す。握りにすると、銀のラインに透明感のある身の白さと血合いの赤が重なって見映えもよい。その景色を楽しんでもらうためにも買ったその晩から出し始め、熟成はかけない。ちなみに、子供の頃には5kgを超える"オオカミ"と呼ばれる大物もよくあった。昨今、流通するのは1〜2kgが主流。それでも天然物に勝るものはない。

This large mackerel with trademark vertical stripes, in its prime from June to August, is most often landed on Japan's Pacific side. Purely wild (as opposed to fish farm escapee) shima-aji are by far the tastiest, especially in the refined sweetness of their dense flesh, distinguished by a pleasant, resilient firmness. Other blue-fish include tender, succulent amberjack, and yellowtail amberjack (hiramasa), which offers clean flavor and a chewy texture, and the taste of shima-aji is somewhere between these. Wild specimens at market are mainly dispatched by ikejime. Choose plump fish fresh of skin, and bright of black eye. The muscle is consistently firm, making the fish easy to fillet, and when the skin is pulled off, the silver tidemark between skin and body remains. Shima-aji nigiri is also visually appealing, this silver line being joined by pale flesh and blood red. I don't age the fish but start serving it the evening after purchase, so diners can enjoy this visual aspect. When I was a boy it was common to see shima-aji over 5kg, but most on the market today weigh 1-2kg. And still nothing beats a wild-caught one.

striped jack

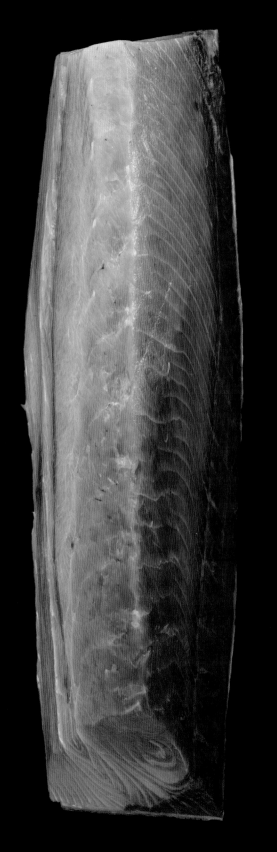

鰤
(buri)

旬は11月後半から1月頃まで。この時季の鰤は"寒鰤"と呼ばれ、冬の味覚の代表格だ。産地は富山の氷見が有名だが、山陰、新潟・佐渡、青森、最近は温暖化の影響で北海道でも良質の鰤が獲れる。身肉はたっぷりと脂を蓄え、他の魚では味わえない鮮烈な甘味を解き放つ。その醍醐味を堪能するには、8kg以上の大きさがあり、皮目に艶があるものを選ぶこと。目玉の周りがこんもりと盛り上がっているものは鮮度がよく、餌を果敢に狙っていたため筋肉質で脂の乗りもことさらよい。刺身であれば、その鮮度が保たれているうちに出すのが定石だ。血合いの真紅が美しく、光沢のある身の弾むような歯触りが満喫できる。ただし、その弾力や脂の強さは握りには不向きだ。父や修業先の親方は「シャリと喧嘩する」と言って鮨ネタに上げなかったほどである。鰤を握りにするためには、熟成が欠かせない。塩で余分な水分を抜いた後、保水紙を毎日取り替えながら1週間ほど寝かせてからようやく出番となる。熟成させた身はしっとり艶めかしく、シャリとの馴染みも上々。チーズに似た熟れた旨味が上がり、獲れたてとはまるで異なる味わいを醸し出すから面白い。

Buri in season from mid-late November to January are dubbed "kan" or "cold-weather" buri, and are a true winter treat. The flesh is divinely fatty, with a striking, unrivalled sweetness. To savor it properly, choose specimens over 8kgs, with lustrous skin. A nice bulge around the eyes indicates freshness, and the fish will be muscled with a good layer of fat, having been boldly hunting its prey. For sashimi it makes sense to serve buri fresh, allowing diners to savor the beautiful bright red of the "chiai" meat close to the spine, and the springy texture of the glistening flesh. That same springiness and sturdy fat however makes buri unsuitable for nigiri, to the extent that both my father, and the head chefs where I trained, declined to use it as a sushi topping, claiming it "fought with the rice." Making nigiri from buri requires aging it first. Salt to remove excess moisture, and leave for a week or so, changing the absorbent paper daily. Only then will it be ready for nigiri, the seductively juicy aged flesh now a perfect partner for sushi rice. Intriguingly, aged buri has an umami similar to cheese, a totally different taste to the freshly caught variety.

Japanese amberjack

間八
(kanpachi)

目の上から背にかけて黒いラインがあり、上から見ると「八」の字に見えるのが名前の由来と言われている。成長に従い名前が変わる出世魚で、成魚の間八は体長1〜2mまで育つ。6月から市場に出回り、秋が深まる10月まで見かける魚だが、最盛期は夏場。なかでも、8月中旬から獲れ始める相模湾産を好んで仕入れている。この時季の相模湾では40cmに満たない "ショッコ" と呼ばれる幼魚も盛んに水揚げされる。軽やかな味わいで脂もすっきりとしているため、こちらも夏の握りの常連だ。選び方は他の青物と同様、体の張りや皮目の光沢を確認する。黒目が澄んだものなら鮮度も間違いないだろう。三枚におろした後、脂の乗りが薄ければ塩を打って水分を調整するが、十分に脂が乗っていればそのまま握りにする。市場では高級魚として名を馳せるだけあって、甘み、旨み、歯応えといずれもバランスは申し分ない。ところが、昨今、間八と聞くとよい顔をしない人が増えている。おそらく養殖物のイメージがあるからだろう。天然物を口にして、あまりの違いに目を見張る人も少なくない。先入観を抜きにして味わってほしい魚の一つである。

Said to be named for the two black lines extending along the fish's back from above the eyes, resembling the character "八" (eight), kanpachi grow to 1-2 meters in length. Appearing at market in June, they are available until October as autumn sets in, but at peak quality in summer. I prefer the Sagami Bay kanpachi caught from mid-August. Most landed at this stage and location are immature specimens under 40cm known as "shokko," which with their light flavor and clean fat, are a regular on the summer nigiri menu. Like other blue-fish, look for a plump, firm body and healthy skin with a lustrous sheen. Add clear eyes, and a fresh fish is guaranteed. Fillet sanmai-oroshi style, and if the fish lacks fat, salt to remove moisture, but if it has a generous layer of fat, it will serve perfectly well unsalted for nigiri. Kanpachi flesh has the ideal balance of sweetness, umami, and firmness one would expect from a premium species. Many these days are put off kanpachi, thinking of the farmed fish; just as many find the taste of wild kanpachi a revelation. A fish worth sampling without preconception.

greater amberjack

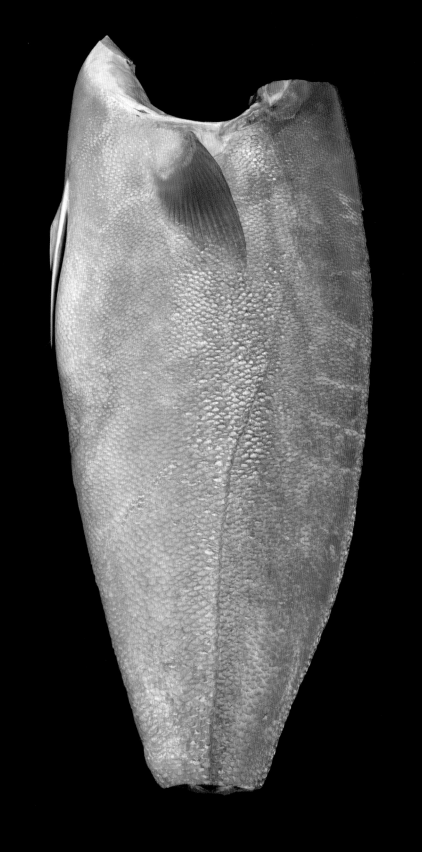

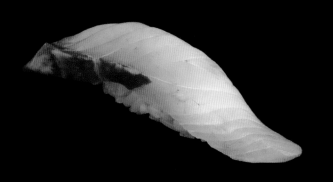

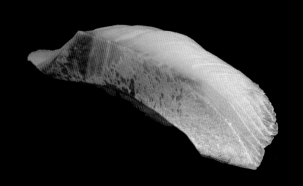

平政
(hiramasa)

精悍な見た目から"海のスプリンター"の異名を取る。旬は6月から7月の2ヵ月ほどと短いが、「冬の鰤、夏の平政」として季節を背負う青物魚だ。鰤に比べて漁獲量は極めて少なく、希少性からも市場では高級魚として名高い。暖かい海域を好み、長崎県の壱岐や島根県の隠岐が名産地として知られ、最近は温暖化の影響で新潟・佐渡でも水揚げされるようになった。仕入れるのは3〜4kgの小ぶりサイズ。目利きをするほど市場に並ばないが、体の中心に真一文字を描く黄金色の線がクリアで、目の色が澄み、尾がピンと伸びていることは確かめる。活け締めがほとんどなので身に張りがあることもポイントだ。さらに、体にこすれた傷がないことは輸送状況の見極めになる。仕入れたら三枚におろし、買った当日から登板となる。血合いの美しさは初日が一番。2〜3日寝かせると舌触りがなめらかになる。塩をあてて寝かしたほうが旨みは上がるが、奥ゆかしい味わいこそ、この魚の本懐。コリッとした歯触りを保ちながらもシャリとよく馴染む身質、噛むと滲み出る淡く上品な甘みと香り。短い旬の記憶として、市場で見つけたら買わずにいられない。

Known as "sea sprinter" for its sleek looks, hiramasa is at markets only during June-July, but nevertheless is tasked with representing the season, as in the saying "buri (yellowtail) for winter, hiramasa for summer." Catches much smaller than buri give hiramasa premium status. I choose smaller specimens weighing 3-4 kg. Though not enough hiramasa turn up at market to test my connoisseurship, I always check that the gold stripes down the body are clear, and the fish's eye color, and that the tail is not drooping. Hiramasa is mainly dispatched by ikejime, so the resulting firm flesh is another trait to look for. Check too for any scratches or scrapes: this tells you how carefully the fish has been transported. Fillet sanmai-oroshi style and serve from the day of purchase. The bloodier flesh will be its most vibrant red on the first day. Age 2-3 days for a smoother palate. Salting and aging does boost umami, but the chief appeal of this fish lies in its refined flavor. With a quality of flesh that complements sushi rice beautifully, while retaining its chewy texture and subtle, refined sweetness and aroma that suffuse the mouth with each bite, hiramasa is a fish I buy whenever I find it.

yellow amberjack

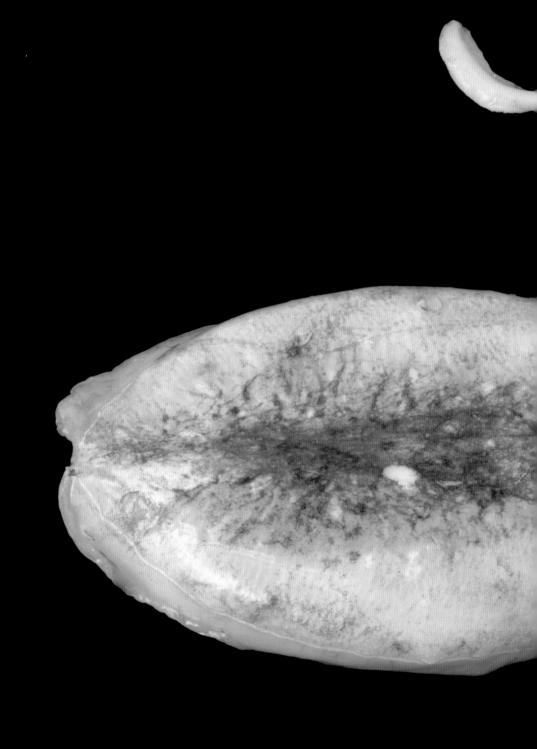

烏賊 ika (squid/cuttlefish)

墨烏賊
(sumi-ika)

胴の中に舟形の甲羅を持つことから甲烏賊とも呼ばれ、冬に味わいを増す烏賊の代表だ。旬の時季は胴の長さが20cm以上になり、身も厚くふくよかになる。雪のような純白の色合いが美しく、シャリシャリとほぐれる歯触りから酢飯との相性もよい。一年中使い続けたいと思うほどだ。名産地は愛知県の渥美半島、兵庫県の淡路島などだが、東京湾で獲れる江戸前の墨烏賊も珍重される。選ぶ際には胴とゲソがつながる2カ所の厚みと、甲羅が外に飛び出していないことを確認。さらに、箱に溜まった墨を触り、さらりとしていれば旨みが身に留まっている確率が高い。仕込みでは熟成が重要になる。捌いた後、保水紙に包んで水分を抜きながら寝かせるほかに、冷凍で熟成させる方法もある。凍らせて48時間以上おくと、ねっとりとして甘みも増す。もう一つのやり方として昆布の間に置くこともある。昆布〆のように圧しはかけず、ふわりと挟む。昆布の風味はつかないが、軽く旨みを入れられる。墨烏賊の握りに合うのは塩とすだちだが、煮切り醤油をひくこともある。ちなみにゲソは握りに向かず、軽く茹でて山葵か黄身醤油でお通しにするのがもっぱらだ。

Best-known of the squid and cuttlefish (both ika in Japanese) species that gain flavor in winter, in season sumi-ika have a thick, spongy body over 20cm long. The crunchiness of the stunning snow-white flesh, falling apart as you chew, makes sumi-ika an excellent match for vinegared rice, good enough in fact to use all year round. When choosing, check the thickness of the torso, and where the legs attach, and that the cuttlebone is not exposed. If ink pooled in the box feels silky smooth, a nice reservoir of umami in the flesh is likely. Aging is a vital part of preparation. After cutting as desired, wrap in moisture-absorbing paper to rest. Freezing is another approach. Frozen for forty-eight hours or more, the flesh will have a succulent sweetness. Sumi-ika can also be placed between sheets of kombu. Sandwich lightly rather than applying kombu-jime pressure. The flavor of the kombu will not linger, just a hint of extra umami. The best complements for sumi-ika nigiri are salt and sudachi, but nikiri sauce is also used. Incidentally, the legs are not suited to nigiri, but should be boiled gently and served with wasabi, or egg yolk marinated in soy sauce, for a mouthwatering appetizer.

golden cuttlefish

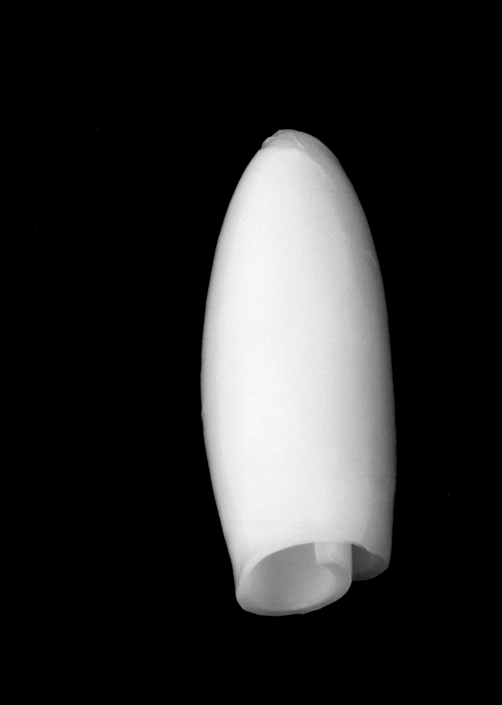

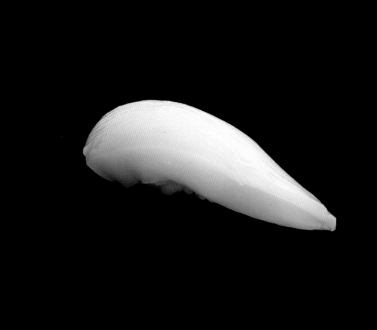

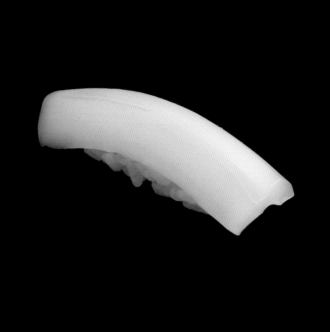

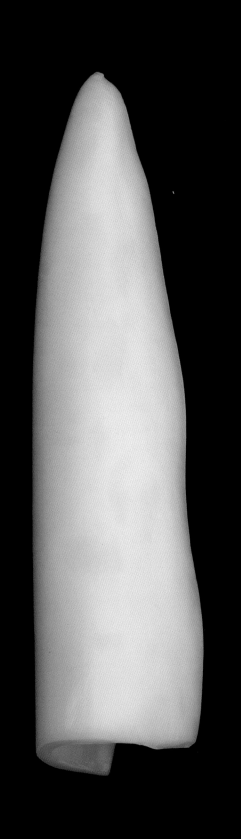

煽烏賊
(aori-ika)

歯を押し返すほどの弾力と噛むほどに湧き上がる鮮烈な甘みから "烏賊の王様" とも称される。漁の最盛期は6〜7月。神奈川、千葉の房総、九州全域で良質のものが獲れる。この烏賊の場合、生きたものを仕入れるのが鉄則だ。といっても、活け物は少なく、氷を張った箱の中から生きているものを探すのである。見極め方は、指で叩くと胴の表面に浮かんだ茶褐色の柄が動くこと、目の周囲にあるブルーが澄んで色が濃いことの2点。大きさは2kg程度がベストだ。烏賊すべてに言えることだが、仕込みでは薄皮を丁寧に剥ぐことが大切である。これにより舌触りが段違いによくなる。ただし、煽烏賊を握りに使うことは稀。強い歯応えはシャリと馴染みにくいからだ。どうしてもと請われれば、表面を薄く削るように切り出した羽衣のような身を数枚重ねて握るが、父や親方には「魚を壊している」と言われかねない。この烏賊においては熟成も適さない。プリッとした歯応えと噛んで楽しむ甘みを損ねてしまうためである。持ち味を堪能するには、薄くそぎ切りなどにしてつまみとして出すのが最適だ。こうした適材適所を見極めるのも鮨屋の仕事なのである。

Resilient firmness and an intense sweetness that grows with every bite have earned aori-ika the title "king of squid." Catches peak in June-July, with high-quality specimens caught in Kanagawa, Bōsō in Chiba, and all around Kyūshū. An ironclad rule with aori-ika is to source it live. In saying this, few are kept in tanks, so it is a matter of looking for live ones among catches packed in ice. The brown markings on the torso will move if tapped, and the clear blue around the eyes will be a dark shade. About 2kg is the right size. Important when prepping any squid is to carefully peel off the membrane, as this will improve the mouthfeel immensely. Aori-ika is rarely used for nigiri, because its robust texture does not go well with rice. If a customer insists, I pile up several thinly-shaved down-like layers to make a nigiri, though my father and old boss would doubtless accuse me of "destroying the fish." Nor does this squid suit aging, which takes away the springy texture and chewy sweetness. The best way to savor the natural flavor of aori-ika is to shave it thinly and serve with drinks. Identifying the best use for an ingredient like this is all part of the sushi chef's job.

bigfin reef squid

達磨烏賊
(daruma-ika)

墨烏賊の入荷が減り始める春半ば、待ってましたとばかりに到来するのが達磨烏賊だ。最盛期は夏。煽烏賊が夏のつまみの定番なら、握りは達磨烏賊の独擅場である。鮨ネタとしては比較的新しいものだが、今や盛夏の風物詩と言えるほどだ。産地は長崎や福岡の九州勢に加え、山口からの入荷も多い。"野地"と呼ばれる発泡スチロールの箱の中から選ぶのは、えんぺらの透明度が高く、目の色が黒々としているもの。赤褐色の胴の色も鮮度の決め手になり、なおかつ胴体が若干の膨らみを持っているかを確認する。煽烏賊より甘みが薄いので、1日置いて旨みを上げることも欠かせない。仕込みについては、薄皮を丁寧に剥いた後、硬い端を取り除いて柵にするところまではほかの烏賊と同様だ。ここから格子状に斜めに包丁目を入れて松笠にし、ごくごく軽く湯通しして握りにすることが多い。松笠にすることで歯切れがよくなり、シャリとしなやかに混ざり合う。もちろん、出で立ちも華やかになり、目を引くこと請け合いだ。開いた笠の上には、ほんの少しの塩とすだち汁を纏わせる。柑橘の清涼感と相俟って、夏らしいさっぱりとした甘みが堪能できる。

Daruma-ika arrive in mid-spring, just as the supply of sumi-ika is declining. Peaking in summer, if aori-ika is the classic summer tsumami (snack), this squid is the unrivaled champion when it comes to nigiri. Though a relatively new sushi topping, it is already a mid-summer menu staple. Kyūshū sources such as Nagasaki and Fukuoka dominate supply, with Yamaguchi also significant. Choose squid with translucent fins and dark black eyes. A reddish-brown torso is another signifier of freshness; also check that the torso is slightly swollen. Daruma-ika is not as intensely sweet as aori-ika, so leave for a day to boost the umami. Prep is the same for other squid up to peeling off the membrane, removing the hard end, and cutting into saku blocks. Next it is common to make diagonal cuts in daruma-ika to form a "pine cone," blanch very briefly, and make into nigiri. The cuts make for a crisper texture, and a more fluid mixing with the vinegared rice. The squid also looks a little more glamorous too of course, never failing to attract attention. Add just a tiny pinch of salt and some sudachi juice to the opened "cone" and savor the magical combo of clean, summery sweetness and refreshing citrus.

swordtip squid

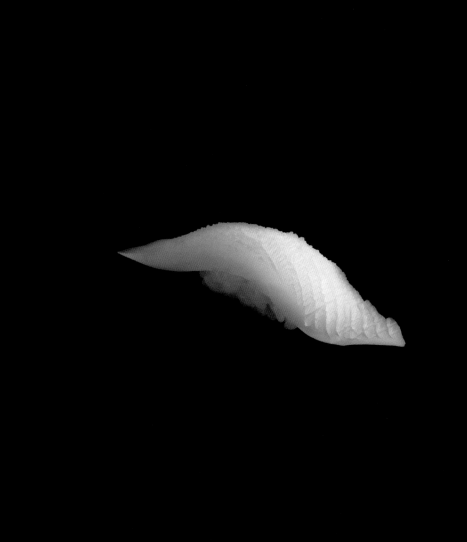

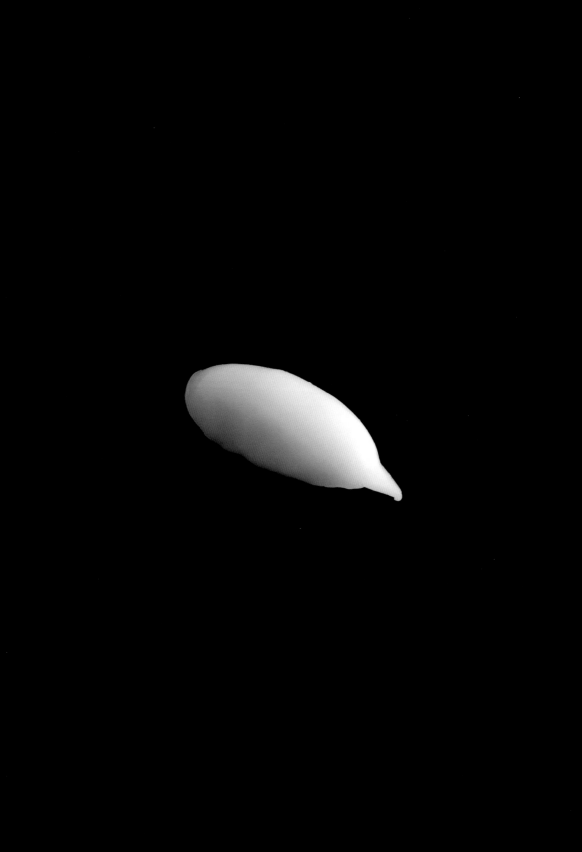

新烏賊
(shin-ika)

新烏賊は墨烏賊の子ども。煽烏賊や達磨烏賊と入れ替わるように登場する鮨屋の夏の風物詩である。かつてはお盆明けに到来したが、昨今は時季が早まり7月後半から見かけるようになった。出始めはワインのコルクの半分ほどの小ささで、1杯で1貫、サイズによっては2杯で1貫を握ることもある。白く薄い身から山葵の淡い緑が透け、涼しげな見た目がいかにも夏らしい。食べ心地は繊細で柔らかく、噛まずとも溶けて儚く消えていく。同じく夏には小肌の新子が出回るが、私の店では新子以上に人気があり、新烏賊の到来を心待ちにする常連客も多い。産地は墨烏賊同様、愛知県・渥美半島、兵庫県・淡路島、鹿児島県・出水や大分をはじめ九州が多く、東京湾でも水揚げされる。網で獲るため潰れやすく、また小さいがゆえに傷みも早い。鮮度がよく、お腹が出ていないなど姿が整ったものを選ぶ必要がある。父や修業先の親方からは「烏賊のゲソは握りに向かない」と教えられてきたが、唯一の例外が新烏賊のゲソだった。くるんと丸まった足の内側につく茶色い皮を柳刃の先で削り取り、くぐらせる程度に軽く茹でてから握る。柔らかくて歯切れがよく、これもまた夏を感じる1貫となる。

Shin-ika are the young of sumi-ika, and a summer sushi staple alongside aori-ika and daruma-ika. Once arriving in mid-August, they are now spotted much earlier, from mid-July. The first are about half the size of a wine cork, enough for a single nigiri, or if smaller, two per nigiri. The refreshing sight of their fine white flesh adorned with the pale, translucent green of wasabi is very summery. Delicate and tender, they melt in the mouth, an ephemeral indulgence. The fry of kohada are also around in summer, but at my restaurant shin-ika is more popular, many regulars looking forward eagerly to its arrival. Being caught in nets, the cuttlefish are easily squashed, and being small, easily damaged. Be sure to choose those that are fresh, and neat in form, without a swollen belly. My father and the chefs I trained with said that squid (cuttlefish) legs were "no good for nigiri," but that shin-ika was the sole exception. Use the tip of a yanagiba sashimi knife to scrape off the brown skin on the inside of the curled-up legs and parboil briefly before making into nigiri that is tender yet robust to the bite, and an authentic taste of summer.

young cuttlefish

煮物 nimono (boiled toppings)

穴子
(anago)

鮪や小肌とともに、江戸前鮨に欠かせないのが煮穴子である。あたかも飲み物のように溶けてなくなり、旨みの余韻だけが残るのが理想。それには産地が重要である。潮の流れが速い外海では筋肉質になり、とろける柔らかさは生まれない。仕入れるのは江戸前・東京湾のみ。特に羽田沖や横浜の野島のものがよい。無数の河川が流れ込む東京湾は、餌となるプランクトンの宝庫。その水を飲むと脂が乗り、身もふっくら厚くなる。とりわけ6月から7月は梅雨の長雨で川底の泥が上がってより栄養は豊かになる。産卵前の穴子にはまさに楽園。だから、江戸前の夏の穴子は旨いのである。市場で買うのは活け物。体の模様が鮮明なものを見繕う。避けたいのは腹がパンパンに膨れたもの。未消化の餌が味に影響するためだ。その場で締めてもらったら、背開きにし、水で洗って徹底的にぬめりを落とす。煮る時間は60〜80分。煮汁は継ぎ足さず、穴子の状態に応じてつくり替える。塩にも合うよう最近は色も味も薄めにしている。仕上げに炙るかどうかは好みである。自分で食べるなら煮汁から取り出したまま握り、穴子の旨みを凝縮させた煮ツメをとろりと纏わせたい。

Boiled anago is an Edomae sushi staple alongside tuna and kohada. Ideally it should dissolve fluidly in the mouth, leaving only a lingering umami afternote. The source of the eel is vital. Out at sea in fast-flowing waters, anago turn tough rather than meltingly tender, so I only buy those from Tokyo Bay, preferably caught off Haneda, or Nojima in Yokohama. Anago before spawning enjoy a varied and fattening diet of plankton from the numerous rivers flowing into Tokyo Bay, making Edomae anago in summer a real treat. Look for live anago at market, choosing those with vivid markings. Avoid any with distended bellies, as undigested food will affect flavor. Have the fishmonger dispatch the eel, then slit open down the back, and rinse thoroughly to remove slime. Boil for 60-80 minutes. Don't add to "mother" broth, but remake for each lot of anago depending on its state. Recently I have been using broth lighter in color and flavor, so the eel will also go with salt. Sear to finish, if preferred. For my own eating, I make nigiri straight out of the broth, served with a dollop of the tsume sauce with its concentrated anago umami.

conger

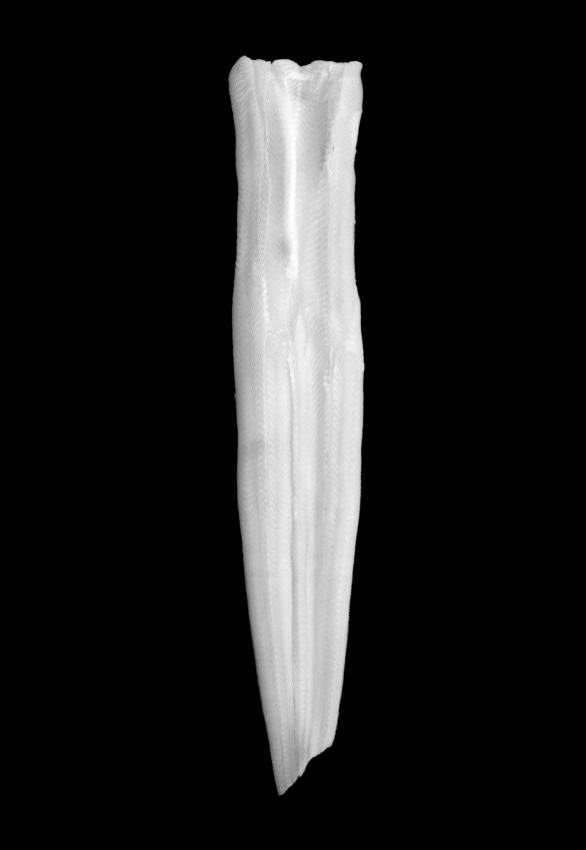

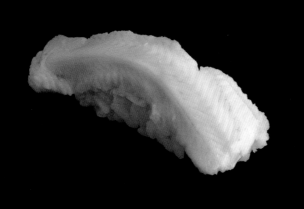

蝦蛄
(shako)

蝦蛄は海老に似た風貌の甲殻類の一種。江戸前鮨では古くから親しまれてきた鮨ネタである。旬は産卵期の初夏、特に梅雨時が最も旨い。「清い水で海老は育たぬ」という格言があるが、蝦蛄も然りである。梅雨の長雨で濁った泥水は栄養の宝庫。この水を飲むことで味わいが増すのである。産地は神奈川県の小柴がつとに知られるが、三河湾や瀬戸内も名産地だ。さらに、最近は小樽など北海道から大型の蝦蛄が入荷し、品質も優れている。市場には活け物も並ぶが浜茹でした物も多く、殻をむいた品も売られている。蝦蛄に限っては必ずしも活け物がよいわけでなく、産地や状態を見て選ぶのが常だ。加えて、雌か雄かも仕入れの判断材料になる。旬の蝦蛄のうち、握りに向くのは雄。しっとり柔らかい身から迸る軽やかな甘みが堪能できる。握りにする場合、茹でた蝦蛄を醤油と酒で味付けした煮汁で軽く煮る"漬け込み"を施し、蝦蛄の煮汁で仕立てた煮ツメを塗るのが昔ながらの江戸前の仕事だ。対して、はち切れんばかりに卵を抱いた雌の蝦蛄は茹でたままつまみにする場合がほとんど。雄に比べて身は薄いものの、ホクホクした卵の味わいは格別の旨さがある。

Shako is a shrimp-like crustacean and longstanding Edomae sushi favorite in season during its early summer spawning, and tastiest during the wet weeks of June-July. There's a saying that "shrimp don't grow in pure water," and this certainly applies to shako, for whom seas muddied by the long rains provide a rich source of nutrients. Imbibing that water gives them a flavor boost. Live shako can be found at market, but also a lot of boiled and shelled specimens. Shako are the one species not always best purchased live, and I usually select by region and condition. Their shrimps' sex is also key: in season, males are better for nigiri, their tender, juicy flesh suffused with a subtle sweetness. The traditional Edomae way to prep shako for nigiri is "tsukekomi" style, taking boiled shako, simmering it briefly in broth seasoned with shōyu and sake, and brushing with tsume sauce made from simmered shako juices. In contrast, female shako bursting with eggs are generally served simply boiled as tsumami. Athough the flesh has less flavor than that of the male, the soft, flaky texture of the roe is a taste sensation in a class of its own.

mantis shrimp

蛸
(tako)

水蛸、柳蛸などの種類があり、鮨屋が主に使うのは身が締まり旨みも濃い真蛸。5月から8月の夏が旬だ。産地は明石が有名だが、鮨ダネには足がむっちり太い太平洋側の蛸が向く。一級品は三浦半島の佐島産。茹でると栗に似た香りが立ち、ミルクのような甘みがある。市場には活け物と浜茹でで並び、その日の状態で選ぶ。店の個性が出るのは活け物の茹で方だ。まず頭を落とし足を1本ずつ分けてから、たっぷりの塩で揉む。泡立つまで丹念に揉むとぬめりが落ち、色よく茹で上がる。叩いて繊維をほぐす工程も欠かせない。ここで使うのは棍棒状にした大根。ジアスターゼにも柔らかくする効果があるようだ。茹でる湯には番茶の葉を入れると、小豆色が濃く歯触りもよくなる。茹で時間は吸盤が小さければ長め、大きければ短めに。足先を上にし吊るして冷ますと、真一文字にのびて旨みも均一に回る。一方、浜茹での蛸は酢水で洗うひと手間によって色も鮮やかになる。握る際はシャリと重なる部分が窪むように波切りにするのがコツ。シャリと馴染んで香りも立ちやすい。煮切り醤油や塩も合うが、火を通したネタには煮ツメを引くのが父の教えだ。

Octopus include mizudako (giant Pacific octopus), and yanagidako (chestnut octopus), but sushi chefs mainly use madako (common octopus) with its firm flesh and intense umami, best from May to August. Both live and boiled are available, and I choose according to condition on the day. My particular way to cook live octopus is to start by taking off the head, then dividing up the legs individually and rubbing with plenty of salt until foaming, to deslime and improve color on boiling. I then beat the flesh to break down the fibers, using a daikon, as apparently the enzyme diastase in the radish has a tenderizing effect. Add bancha tea leaves to the boiling water for a darker russet color and superior texture. Boil longer for small suckers, and vice versa. Hang legs by tips to cool and extend, which also equalizes the umami. Pre-boiled octopus can be simply washed in diluted vinegar to achieve a more vibrant color. When making nigiri, the trick is to cut corrugations so that parts in contact with the rice bed in securely. Octopus goes well with sushi rice, which adds to its perfume. Nikiri sauce or salt suit octopus, but my father taught me to brush tsume sauce on cooked octopus toppings.

octopus

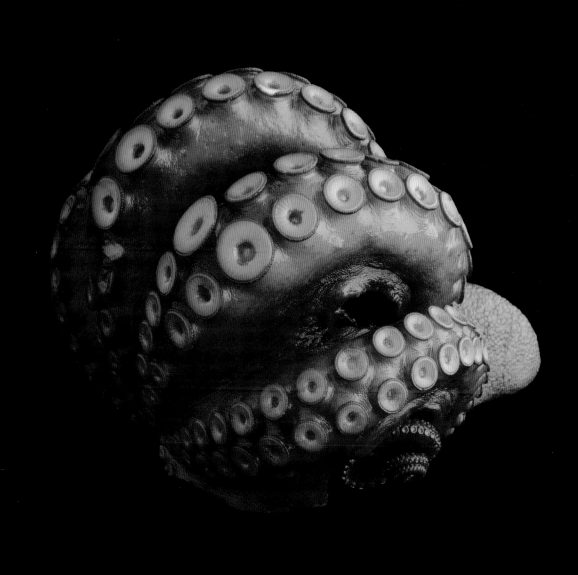

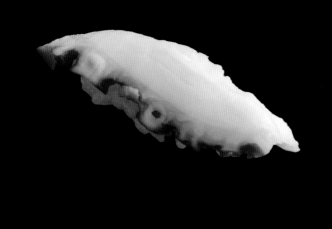

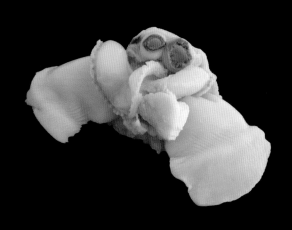

蛤
(hamaguri)

蛤は江戸前伝統の鮨ネタだ。この貝に限っては生で食べず、漬け込みという手法で煮蛤にしてから握る。通年出すネタだが、特に旨いのは産卵前の3月から5月。身がぷっくり太って食べ応えがある。仕入れるのは千葉・九十九里や茨城・鹿嶋の地蛤だ。日本の固有種で、外来種と違って火を入れても柔らかい。生きた貝であることも仕入れの絶対条件だ。その上で殻がしっかり閉じて持ち重りのするものを選ぶ。買って帰り剥き身にしたら、まず行うのが砂出しである。貝が呼吸や摂食に使う水管に5〜6本の串を通し、くるくる回しながら水洗いすると砂を除ける。身を傷めないよう配慮した江戸前独特の手法だ。これに続くのが茹で。沸騰した湯に塩ひとつまみと剥き身の蛤を入れ、再び沸いたらすぐに引き上げて余熱で火を通す。硬くなるので茹で過ぎは禁物。タイミングがすべてだ。冷めたら剥き身を開いてわたを取り除き、蛤の茹で汁に調味料を加えた漬け地に浸せば仕込みは完了だ。握るのは味が染みた3日目以降。むちっとした身は噛むほどに濃厚な旨みが溢れ、蛤の煮ツメの甘みがアクセントになる。大切に守りたい伝承の1貫である。

Hamaguri is a traditional Edomae sushi topping and the only shellfish not eaten raw but gently poached, using a marinating technique known as tsukekomi. Served all year round, the clams are especially tasty from March to May before spawning, when their meat is delectably plump. Endemic to Japan, hamaguri remain soft even when cooked, unlike imported varieties. Buy live clams, firmly closed, and fairly heavy. Shell and purge of sand by inserting 5-6 skewers into the clam's feeding and respiration tubes, turning the skewers while rinsing, a special Edomae technique to avoid damaging the flesh. Next is boiling: add a pinch of salt and the cleaned clams to boiling water, and when the water returns to the boil, take off the heat immediately and leave in pot to finish cooking. Never overcook as this makes the clams tough. Once cooled, splay open, remove intestines, and marinate in seasoned cooking liquid. Use in nigiri from the third day onward, once the flavor has permeated. Each bite of the plump, juicy flesh brings another blast of intense umami, accented by sweet tsume sauce made from the cooking liquid. This is one tradition definitely worth continuing.

common Orient clam

浅利

(asari)

浅利は蛤と同じく江戸前らしい鮨ネタだ。弾力があり旨みも濃厚な煮蛤に比べ、煮浅利はあっさりとして食べ心地は軽やか。小粋で庶民的なところも好ましく、店でも度々握りの一つに加えている。最近の若い鮨屋ではあまり見かけないが、浅草辺りの昔ながらの店では受け継がれているようである。煮物にするには粒が大きいほどよく、長年、愛知・三河産一辺倒だ。旬は春と秋の2回あり、これらの時季に出番はおのずと増える。仕込みは煮蛤と同様、江戸前伝統の漬け込みである。ただし、その仕事には相当の気合いと根気が必要だ。小さな二枚貝を1つずつ剥き、細い水管に串を差したら水をあてながらくるくる回して砂抜きをする。さっと茹でて冷ましたらそれぞれ開いてわたを取り除くのである。漬け地は浅利の茹で汁に醤油、酒、味醂で調味。最低でも1日漬けて味を含ませてから握りにして煮ツメを塗る。1貫に使う浅利は3〜4粒。滑り落ちないように握るのも職人の腕の見せ所だ。小粒の貝ゆえにどう頑張っても1日10貫出せるかどうか。手間と時間はかかるものの、付け台に置いたときの粋な風情を目にするとまた仕込もうと思えてくる。

Like hamaguri, asari are a classic Edomae sushi topping. Asari are lighter eating than the firm, intensely flavorful hamaguri, and their winning combination of style plus lack of pretention makes them a regular on my nigiri menu. Less favored by today's young sushi chefs, they seem to feature more at older establishments around Asakusa. Asari have two seasons, spring and autumn. Like hamaguri, preparation is by traditional Edomae tsukekomi, but requiring extra patience and effort, as each tiny bivalve has to be shelled and purged of sand using skewers under running water. Boil quickly, and once cool, splay open and remove intestines. Make a marinade using the asari cooking juices, soy sauce, sake, and mirin, and steep for at least a day to allow flavors to absorb, before forming into nigiri and brushing over tsume. Use 3-4 asari for each piece of sushi. Keeping the clams on the rice is a test of the chef's skill. The small size of these shellfish means I can serve ten pieces of asari nigiri per day at the most. Despite the effort involved, each time one is set on the counter, its stylish appearance always makes me want to do another.

Japanese littleneck clam

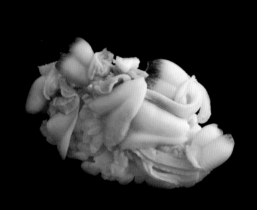

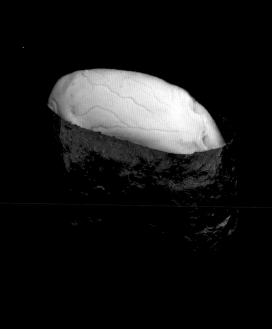

牡蠣

(kaki)

牡蠣はつまみとしてはもちろん、握りにしても生きるネタである。つまみの場合はそのまま生牡蠣として供するが、握りには煮牡蠣が合う。煮ると言っても濃い味で煮含めるのでなく、醤油と酒を加えた薄味のだしで軽く火を入れるのみ。うっすら味を含ませたその煮牡蠣を軍艦巻きにし、牡蠣の煮汁でつくった煮ツメを塗るのが定番だ。海苔の香りと煮ツメの甘みが牡蠣の味を一段引き上げてくれる。店で出すのは10月から2月の5ヵ月ほど。仕入れるのは北海道東部、厚岸産の丸牡蠣と決めている。野付半島の先でオホーツク海と太平洋の海流がぶつかるこの海域はプランクトンが多く、肥えた海が良質の牡蠣を育ててくれる。古くから牡蠣の産地と知られ、地名はアイヌ語の「アッケシシ(牡蠣の多いところ)」に由来するという説もあるほどだ。買うのは市場に到着したての鮮度がよいもので、殻がしっかりと閉じてずっしり重いもの。丸々と太った牡蠣はプリッと弾力があり、頬張るとミルクに似たコクのある旨みとほのかな磯の香りがまろやかに広がる。厚岸産ならではのクリーミーな味わいがあってこそ、煮牡蠣の握りは本領を発揮できるのである。

Oysters make superb tsumami, but a great nigiri topping too. Raw is best when serving with drinks, but cooked is better suited to nigiri. By cooked I don't mean poached with intense flavor, but in a light stock with the addition of shōyu and sake. The classic way to serve these oysters with a hint of extra flavor is as gunkan-maki, brushed with tsume sauce made from the simmering juices. The fragrance of the nori and sweetness of the sauce take the flavor of the oyster to another level. I serve oysters for about five months from October to February, always from Akkeshi in eastern Hokkaidō. The waters beyond the Notsuke Peninsula where the Sea of Okhotsk meets the Pacific are teeming with plankton, fertile feeding grounds for fine oysters. Long renowned for these deliciously creamy mollusks, Akkeshi is said by some to take its name from the Ainu "akkeshin" meaning "place with lots of oysters." I buy fresh oysters newly arrived at market, heavy and with shells firmly shut. Meat for the ultimate oyster nigiri, these plump Akkeshi morsels are firm to the bite and release an intense, milky umami and briny aroma that suffuse and delight the palate.

oyster

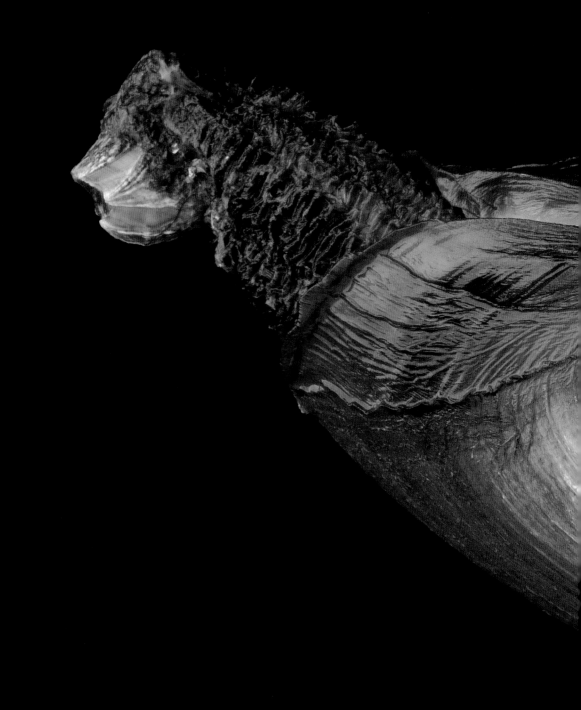

貝 kai (shellfish)

海松貝

(mirugai)

本海松貝、黒海松貝の呼び名もあるが、正式名称は海松食。二枚貝から伸びた太い水管に海松という海藻がつき、それを食べているように見えることから名付けられたという。旬は春と秋の2回。産地には瀬戸内や東京湾があるが、最近は三河湾産がほとんどだ。漁獲量は総じて減り、希少性から高級品になっている。ちなみに、巷でよく見る白海松貝はまったく別の貝だ。代替品が出回るほど希少ということだろう。選び方は生きた貝で大きく重いものがよい。触れた瞬間、水管をぴゅっと引っ込めるほど元気なら申し分ない。握りにするのはこの水管だ。殻から出し、水管からワタ、ヒモ、貝柱を外したら、沸騰した湯に2〜3秒くぐらせる。氷水で冷まして黒い皮を剥ぐと乳白色の中身が現れる。2つに割って塩を打ち、汗をかいたら拭き取って冷蔵庫で休ませてから握る。毎度、見惚れるのは出で立ちの美しさだ。乳白色の端が紫がかり、なんとも風情がある。シコシコと歯触りもよく、噛むほどに潮の香りと澄んだ甘みが湧き上がる。人気の高いネタであり、海松下と呼ぶ水管の付け根も握りにすると喜ばれる。ヒモや小柱は軽く炙ると酒のつまみに格好だ。

Mirugai go by various names, but are properly called mirukui, from the seaweed called miru which attaches to their thick siphon as if they are eating it (kui). In season spring and autumn. Found in various locations, but these days mainly sourced from Mikawa Bay in Aichi. An overall decline in catches has made mirugai a rare delicacy. Note that the shiro (white) mirugai seen around markets are a different species. Choose live clams that are large and heavy, all the better if they quickly retract their siphon at your touch. Shell the clam, remove viscera, himo and adductor muscle, and plunge into boiling water for 2-3 seconds. Cool in ice water and peel off the black skin to reveal the milky flesh. Split in two, salt, wipe when the flesh starts to sweat, and rest in refrigerator before making into nigiri. The sheer showiness of mirugai delights me every time, the edges of the milky-white meat taking on a lovely purple tinge. Each springy bite and mastication releases an aroma of the sea, and unadulterated sweetness. A popular topping, with nigiri made from the root of the siphon also sure to please. Grilled, the himo and adductor muscle make delicious tsumami.

mirugai clam

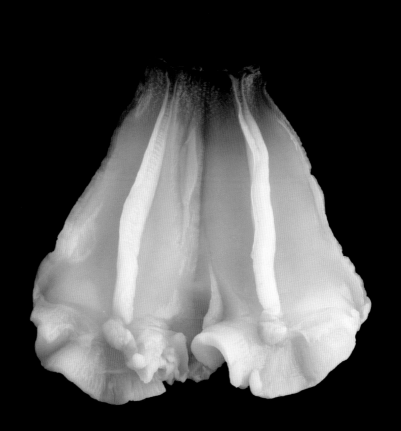

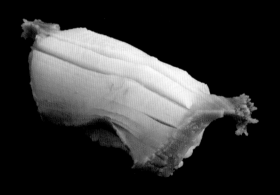

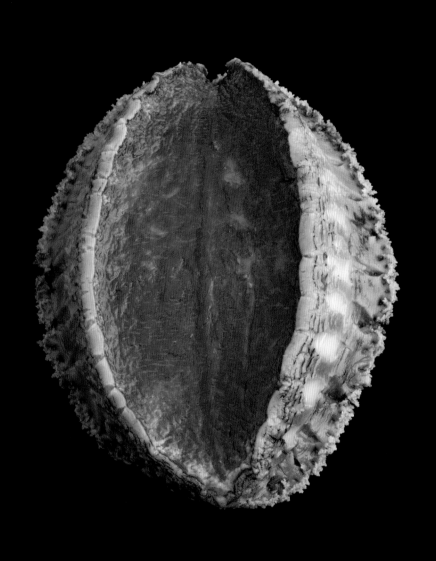

鮑
(awabi)

新緑の季節に旬を迎え10月頃まで続く。生で食べるなら黒鮑、蒸すなら眼高鮑というのが鮨屋でのすみ分けだ。どちらも千葉・大原産が最高峰。大きくて殻が薄く、水槽にへばりついて取るのに苦労するぐらい活きのよいものを選ぶ。握りに使う眼高鮑は質の高いものほど大きく800gから1kgに及ぶ。身の表面が枇杷色をしたものが旨く、市場では「枇杷っ貝」と珍重される。父は「枇杷が腐る寸前の色が最高だ」と言っていた。鮑の仕込みは独特で、殻のままどさっと塩をあてるのが最初の工程だ。暴れる鮑が落ち着いたら揉み、殻を外してよく洗う。この後、肝も一緒に酒を振りかけ蒸すこと3〜4時間。1時間おきに酒をかけ、蒸す間に出た汁に浸して保存する。蒸し立てはミルクに似た香りが湯気の中から立ち上がる。飴色の身は柔らかく、噛んだときのふくよかな甘みと香りは蒸し鮑ならでは。切り付けはシャリ側を波切りにし、シャリと密着させるのがコツ。肝はつまみが多いが、薄く切り握りに載せるのもオツだ。食べ方は塩、煮切り醤油、穴子の煮ツメから好みで。冬に鮑を所望されると岩手・三陸の蝦夷鮑を蒸して握るが、それもまた旨い。

Awabi reach their prime to coincide with the fresh green growth of spring, and continue to around October. At sushi restaurants, black abalone are for eating raw, and madaka abalone steamed. The finest of both come from Ōhara in Chiba. Madaka for nigiri are of best quality at weights from 800g up to 1kg. The tastiest and most prized have a golden loquat-colored surface to their flesh. My father always said the very best were "the color of an almost-rotten loquat." Abalone require some special prepping. The first step is to dredge with salt, and once the startled abalone has settled, knead, shell and wash thoroughly. Next, sprinkle with sake, including the liver, and steam for 3-4 hours, adding more sake every hour, then store in the steaming liquid. The amber flesh will be tender, with the generous succulence and aroma characteristic of steamed abalone. When cutting, make corrugations on the rice side so the flesh will adhere. The liver is often served as a snack, but thinly cut, makes a great nigiri topping. Season to taste with salt, nikiri sauce, or the tsume sauce of anago. If abalone is requested in winter I steam Ezo abalone from the Sanriku coast of Iwate, which makes superb nigiri.

abalone

鳥貝
(torigai)

なめらかな舌触り、シャリシャリとした歯切りのよさ、そして軽やかな甘みとほどよい磯の香りが鳥貝の持ち味だ。握りに使うのは黒い足の部分。その形が鳥の嘴に似ているのが名前の由来である。旬は3月からゴールデンウィークが終わるまで。春限定の貝の一つだ。仕入れるのは東京湾、三河湾、伊勢湾、舞鶴のいずれか。持ち重りがして、触った瞬間に動けば活きのよい証拠だ。生食もできるが、軽く湯通しすると甘みが増す。殻から取り出しワタを海水で掃除したら、沸騰した湯に落として6〜7秒。一度に入れると加減が狂うため、一つずつ湯にくぐらせるのが鉄則だ。捌き方にもコツがある。使うのはまな板でなくガラス板だ。"お歯黒"と呼ばれる黒く艶やかな色はこの貝の取り柄。少し擦れただけで色落ちするため、摩擦の少ないガラス板で慎重に捌く必要がある。鳥の嘴のように尖った先がピンと立つように握ると美しい。そのために捌いた当日に使い切るようにしている。もっとも、生きた鳥貝を扱う鮨屋はさほど多くなく、剥いて湯引きしたものを買うほうが一般的だ。冷凍品も多く、そうなると味は別物。鳥貝にとっては不本意なことだろう。

Torigai offers a smooth texture, chew with a hint of crunch, subtle sweetness, and perfect tang of the ocean. Nigiri is made from the dark-colored foot, similar in form to the beak of a bird (tori), hence the name. Available from March to the end of Golden Week (May), torigai is a treat exclusive to spring. Though edible raw, a quick blanching boosts sweetness. Shell, use seawater to clean out viscera, and drop into boiling water for 6-7 seconds. Always do one at a time: all at once, and results will vary too much. Another trick to handling torigai is to use a glass plate rather than the usual chopping board. A strong point of this shellfish is its glossy black coloring, known as "ohaguro" (teeth blackening). The slightest rub can remove this, so careful handling on relatively frictionless glass is required. Nigiri made with the beak-like tip upright is pertly pretty, and to achieve this the shellfish must be used the day it is processed by the chef. Few sushi restaurants deal in live torigai, preferring to buy in peeled and parboiled specimens. Frozen torigai are also common, though not at all as good, and to mind, almost disrespectful to the shellfish.

Japanese cockle

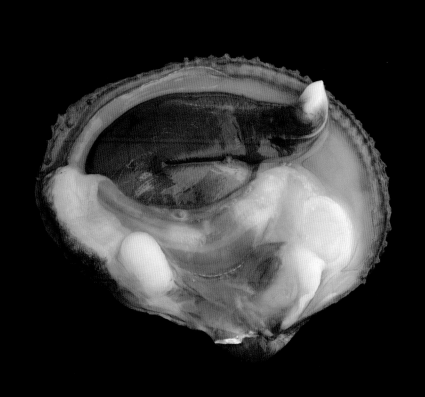

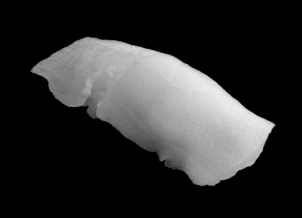

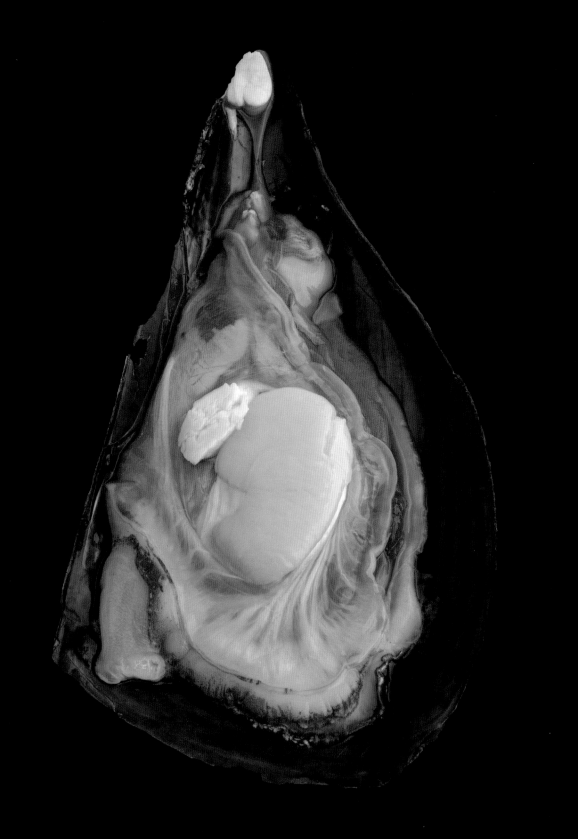

平貝
(tairagai)

内湾などの砂泥底に生息する平貝は、長さ30cm以上に育つ大型の二枚貝。帆立貝と同様、中心にある貝柱が鮨ダネになる。旬は11月から4月と長く、主な産地は三河湾や熊本県・天草。他の貝と同じく、生きているものを買うのが大前提だ。加えて、貝柱ができるだけ太く透明感があるものを選ぶ。仕込みはシンプルだ。殻から取り出した貝柱の周りに軽く塩を打ち、汗をかいたら水洗いして冷蔵庫で休ませる。ヒモや肝などは食べることもできるが、さほど旨いものではないので使うことはない。握りにする場合、切り付けはやや薄めに、シャリの形に沿うよう包丁を入れる。するとシャリと密着するので海苔の帯を巻く必要がなく、その分、貝の味わいを素直に楽しめる。つまみでは煮切り醤油を塗りながら焼き、海苔でくるりと巻いた磯辺焼きも人気がある。生のときはもちもちとして、焼くとサクサクと歯切れがよくなり、その食感の変化も楽しい。クセがないので食べやすく、甘みや香りも淡白で上品。万人に好まれる味わいである。昨今、鮨屋では帆立貝のほうがポピュラーだが、父の時代には帆立貝より平貝をよく使ったと聞く。これも時代なのだろう。

A large bivalve that grows to over 30cm, found in sandy inlets. Like the scallop, the central adductor muscle is the part used in sushi. The season is long, from November to April, with primary sources being Mikawa Bay, and Amakusa in Kumamoto. Like other shellfish, the key is to buy live. Choose specimens with the fattest, clearest adductors. Tairagai are easy to prep: salt lightly around the adductor removed from the shell, and when it sweats, rinse with water and refrigerate. The himo, liver and so on are also edible, but not especially tasty so I don't bother with them. To make nigiri, slice slightly thin to fit the shape of the rice, helping it to adhere, and doing away with the need for a nori wrapping to permit pure pleasure in the taste of the shellfish. For tsumami, grill, brushing with nikiri sauce, and wrap in nori for a popular isobeyaki bite. The change in texture is another delight: doughy raw, and crispy cooked. Mild and easy to eat, with its subtle, refined sweetness and aroma, tairagai is a universal favorite. Scallops are now more popular for sushi, but in my father's day, tairagai ruled. Another sign that times change, I guess.

pen shell

青柳
(aoyagi)

橙色の美しい身を持つこの貝の正式名称は"バカ貝"。由来は諸説あり、その昔、東京湾でバカのように獲れたからというのが通説だ。とはいえ、あまりにかわいそうだとかつて一大集積地だった千葉県・市原の地名から青柳の呼び名がついたと伝えられている。最盛期は12月下旬から5月中旬。現在も東京湾産は多く、ほかに伊勢湾や北海道も主産地だ。市場に並ぶ大半が殻を外した剥き身。指で触れると身を縮める新鮮なものから大きな剥き身を見繕う。買って帰ったらまずは水を張ったボウルに入れ、くるくるとかき混ぜて水洗いをする。ざるに上げて水を切り、再び水を張り替えたボウルへ……と繰り返すこと6回。ヒモは一緒に握るので、取れると見映えが悪くなる。極力触らずに洗うことが大切だ。この後、沸騰した湯で2秒ほど湯通しをする。わずか2秒だが、強い磯の香りが和らいで味わいはぐっと洗練されるから欠かせない。ワタは開いて取り除き、ヒモの薄い膜はピンセットで剥がす。細部まで丁寧にしなければ、研ぎ澄まされた美しさは生まれない。握ったら煮切り醤油とともにすだちを少々。ツノがピンと立った姿は赤貝に負けない艶っぽさがある。

The proper name for these shellfish with stunning orange flesh is "bakagai" or "stupid" (baka) shellfish. A common theory behind the name is that they were once caught in stupidly (baka ni) large quantities in Tokyo Bay. Even so, it is said they were given the name aoyagi out of pity, after the Chiba location where they were most concentrated. Peaking from late December to mid-May, most in markets are shelled specimens. Choose a large one from those fresh enough to flinch at your touch. Place in a bowl of water, stir around, drain, and repeat with fresh water... six times in all. The himo is included in nigiri, so leave intact for visual effect, taking care not to touch it while washing. Blanch the flesh for about two seconds, a short but vital step as it will mitigate the strong briny odor, making for a far more refined flavor. Open up and remove viscera, then use tweezers to take the thin membrane from the himo. Every step must be performed with minute precision to create aoyagi's finely honed attractiveness. Season nigiri with nikiri sauce and a little sudachi. The sight of aoyagi with its "horn" (foot) proudly erect rivals akagai in terms of sushi sex appeal.

Chinese mactra clam

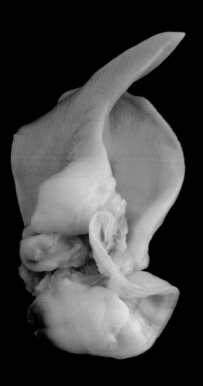

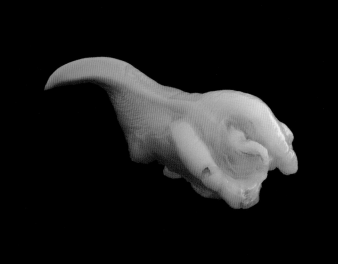

赤貝
(akagai)

鮨屋が扱う貝類のなかで、格上とされるのが赤貝である。気品に満ちた朱色の貝が付け台に上がるとカウンターが一気に華やぐ。格という点では鮑を凌ぐほどだ。最盛期は秋から春まで。仕入れは宮城県・閖上産の一択である。豊潤な旨み、鮮烈な磯の香り、小気味よい歯応え。どれをとっても申し分ない。閖上産以外を使ったのは東日本大震災後の数年間だけ。現在も完全に戻ったとは言えないが、やはり閖上に勝る産地はないとさえ思う。買うのは当然、殻付きの活け物だ。手に持ちずっしり重いことを確認する。仕込みに取り掛かるのは開店時間が迫ってきたとき。早くに仕込むと風味が抜けてしまうからだ。仕込み方にもコツがある。殻から出したときに出てくる血の赤い汁をボウルに溜め、むいた貝はその中に浸ける。肝やヒモを外す際も、あえてまな板に赤い汁を溜めながら進めていく。こうすると鮮度が落ちにくいのである。剥いた後、塩でアクを落とす工程も欠かせない。握る前には放射状に細かく包丁を入れ、8の字に握ると見映えがし、縁起もよいとされている。ヒモは握りや巻き物、酢の物に。肝は醤油味の煮付けにすると格好のお通しになる。

Akagai enjoys star status among sushi shellfish. The appearance on the counter of this graceful scarlet mollusk surpassing even abalone for sheer class, always causes a stir. Peaking in quality from autumn to spring, for me, akagai can have just one source: Yuriage in Miyagi. Umami-rich, intensely briny, and delightfully springy to the bite, it is a superb choice for all these reasons. Naturally, I purchase it live in the shell. Weigh each specimen in your hand to check it feels heavy. I leave prepping akagai almost until opening time; any earlier risks loss of flavor. Catch the red blood that comes out when akagai is shelled, and steep the flesh in it. Keep some of this red liquid on the board when removing the liver and himo (mantle) too, as this helps to maintain freshness. After shelling, salt to dispel sliminess. Make a series of radial cuts in the flesh before forming into figure-eight, a visually stunning piece of nigiri also deemed auspicious. The himo is used in nigiri, makimono, or vinegared, while the liver of akagai, blanched with shōyu flavoring, makes a tempting appetizer.

blood cockle

帆立貝

(hotate-gai)

主役は貝の真ん中にある貝柱。昨今、鮨ネタとして人気が高く、養殖も盛んだ。それも悪くはないが、仕入れとなれば別。買うのは北海道・野付半島の天然物、これ一筋である。一線を画すのはまず大きさだ。4〜5年物が中心のため、貝殻は女性の顔ほどのジャンボサイズ。活きのよさも抜群で、仕入れ帰りの車中ではカスタネットのような音が鳴り響く。貝柱は最大で10㎝ほどと分厚く、飴色がかった乳白色の色合いに風格が漂う。歯応えと甘みはもはや別物だ。帆立貝というと柔らかいイメージがあるが、野付産は弾力が強く、シャリシャリと心地よくほぐれる。甘みも菓子に近いぐらい鮮烈だ。旬は12月から5月だが、ピークは桜咲く4月頃。別次元の旨さには驚くばかりである。仕込みはシンプルで、殻を外しヒモとワタを取り除くのみ。握りには横に開いてまるごと一つをつける。厚みを持たせて握ると豊潤な甘みを存分に堪能できる。刺身は歯応えが強調されるよう縦に切る。少しの塩で十分な旨さだ。帆立貝は元来、江戸前鮨にはなく、父は頑なに握らなかった。暖簾とともに父の流儀を継承したが、意を翻したのは野付の天然物に出会ったからにほかならない。

Sushi scallop offerings center on the shellfish's central adductor muscle. A popular topping these days, many scallops are also farmed. All well and good, but I confess I use solely wild scallops from Hokkaidō's Notsuke Peninsula. Size is the first clue when buying: most scallops at market are 4-5 years old, so have a shell about the size of a woman's face. The best will also be lively critters that clatter like castanets on the drive home. The adductor will be a sturdy up to 10cm thick, and an elegant, amber-tinged milky shade. The season runs from December to May, peaking around April cherry blossom time, when the flavor moves into another, even more astounding realm. Prep is simple: just shell and remove viscera and himo. For nigiri, open horizontally and use whole. A thick topping allows full appreciation of the scallop's rich sweetness. Cut vertically for sashimi, where bite is more important. A touch of salt is all the seasoning you need. Scallops are not a traditional Edomae topping, and my father stubbornly refused to serve them. I may have inherited Dad's way of doing things along with the business, but on this one point, the scallops of Notsuke changed my mind.

scallop

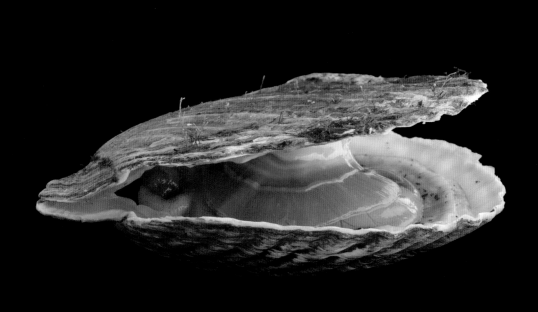

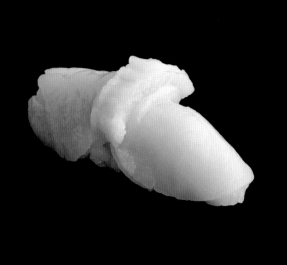

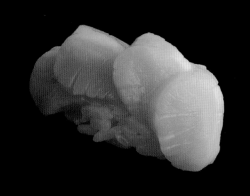

小柱
(kobashira)

冬から初夏にかけて味わいを増す青柳は、貝柱の旨さにも定評がある。小柱はこの青柳の貝柱の呼称だ。ゆえに産地は青柳と同じ東京湾、伊勢湾、北海道が中心。市場では殻から取り出した小柱が身とは別に並ぶが、買うのは"大星"と決めている。そもそも青柳は大小2つの貝柱を持ち、大星とは大きい柱を指す。小さい柱は小星と呼び、それぞれ選り集めて売られている。大星のほうが値は張るが、大粒ならではの食べ応えが堪能できる。甘みや香りも豊かで品があり、さっくりとした歯触りも小気味よい。持ち帰ったら特に仕込みはなく、鮨屋にとってはラクなネタだ。ただし、握りにするにはひと工夫がいる。そのまま握ればシャリからポロポロこぼれて、食べにくいことこの上ない。そのため軍艦巻きにする店は多いが、海苔の風味が小柱の繊細な味わいを邪魔するのが難点だ。海苔を使わずに見映えよく握るには半分に開くこと。据わりがよくなり、手でも箸でもスマートに口にできる。もちろん、開いても十分な厚みはほしい。大星を選ぶのはそのためでもある。小柱の握りは人気があり青柳を凌ぐほど。握る度、青柳にはいささか申し訳ない気持ちになる。

Acquiring flavor from winter through to early summer, aoyagi are also known for their delectable adductor muscles, known as kobashira. At market kobashira taken from the shell are presented separately to aoyagi flesh, and I always buy the larger of the clam's two adductors, known as the "ōboshi" (big star). The smaller is the "koboshi" or "little star" and the two are grouped separately for sale. The ōboshi costs more, but its size makes it a more satisfying feast. It is also sweet, fragrant and refined, with a pleasingly light texture. An easy, no-prep option for sushi chefs, it does however require a little ingenuity to use in nigiri. Placed on rice as is, it will fall off in a most frustrating fashion. Many restaurants get around this by making it into gunkan-maki, the problem with this being that the taste of the nori can eclipse the kobashira's delicate flavor. To make into attractive nigiri sans nori, open out into halves. This will make it easier to handle by hand or chopsticks. You still want plenty of thickness, which is why I choose ōboshi. Kobashira nigiri is even more popular than the aoyagi flesh itself: I always feel I'm doing the poor clam a disservice...

clam muscle

北寄貝
(hokkigai)

本来、江戸前の鮨ネタにはなく、握るようになったのは5年ほど前。きっかけは北海道・長万部産の黒北寄貝との出会いにある。豊穣の海として名高い噴火湾で育った黒北寄貝は、名前の通り、殻が黒みがかり、大きくて厚みもふくよか。シャリシャリした独特の歯応えも抜群だ。仲買人に紹介されたのだが、北寄貝の概念を覆す味わいにびっくりしたことを覚えている。旬は12月後半から3月頃までの寒い時期。ほかの貝同様、ずしっと持ち重りのするものを買うと、殻の中にびっしりと身が詰まっている。仕込みでは殻を開くとき以外、一切、包丁は使わない。指先とピンセットを使って、身を傷めないよう丁寧にワタなどを掃除していく。このとき、身の内側にあるヒダの部分をできるだけ多く残すよう心がけている。ヒダのところに甘みがあるからだ。さらに、握る前には片面だけほんの数秒、湯通しする。生で握る店もあるが、軽く熱をあてたほうが口当たりがしなやかになる。もともと大きな貝なので、1貫に対して半身で十分。裏返してヒダを見せるように握り、煮切り醤油をひくと凹凸のある表面に醤油がパーッと散って見惚れるほどの美しさだ。

In season from late December to March or so, hokkigai is not a traditional Edomae topping, and is one I only started using about five years ago. Black hokkigai from Hokkaidō's Funka (Uchiura) Bay, renowned for its fertile waters, does indeed have a black shell, and is large and fleshy, with a distinctive crunchy texture. I was introduced to this variety by a wholesaler, and remember being surprised by how it challenged my preconceptions of hokkigai. Like other shellfish, hokkigai with heft are reliably crammed with meat. When prepping, avoid using a knife apart from opening the shell. Use tweezers and fingertips to carefully clean out the viscera without damaging the flesh. I am always careful to retain as much of the tasty pleating in the flesh as possible. Before making into nigiri, rinse just one side in boiling water for just a few seconds, to create a more supple mouthfeel. These are big clams, so half of one per piece of nigiri is sufficient. Turn over to top the nigiri, to show off the pleats. A coating of nikiri sauce will swiftly disperse across the bumpy surface, adding to the spectacle. Who knew a mere clam could be so seductive?

surf clam

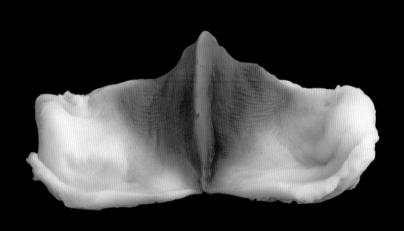

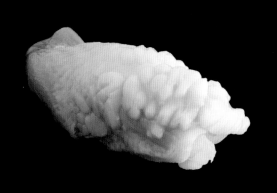

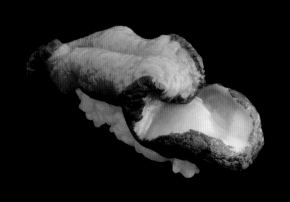

栄螺

(sazae)

夏の鮑に先駆けて登場するのが栄螺である。磯焼きでお馴染みの巻貝だが、生で握っても軽い歯ごたえがシャリに合い、優しい甘みと磯の香りが楽しめる。旬は4月から7月。大原、御宿、白浜といった千葉の外房産をメインに仕入れる。特に大原のものは品質がよく、市場でも人気が高い。仕入れるのは生きた貝で、殻が薄く、大きくて重いもの。500g～700gあれば、一つで2、3貫握ることができる。ちなみに、殻から伸びるツノは潮の流れが速いと長く、穏やかなら短くなる。ツノの短いものは時化の日に獲ると旨いなどと言われるが、さほど味の違いはないようだ。蓋を取り殻から出したら、身、貝柱、肝に切り分ける。身は塩を振りもみ洗いしてぬめりと汚れを取り除く。風味を損ねるので洗いすぎは禁物だ。握る際には観音開きに開いて隠し包丁を入れて歯切れをよくするのもコツ。煮切り醤油をひきすだちを搾ると、爽やかな酸味が貝の甘みを引き立てる。もちろん、刺身にも向き、肝と貝柱は殻に戻して焼くと絶好のつまみになる。栄螺の肝は苦味が強いものが多いが、仕入れる品は甘くてまろやか。鮑の肝に匹敵する旨さである。

Sazae appears ahead of summer abalone. A turban shell frequently on the isobeyaki menu, it can also be used raw in nigiri; the light crunch a superb match for sushi rice, and the mild sweetness and sea scent making the mouth sing. The season runs from April to July. Buy live specimens, big and heavy with thin shells. A 500-700g sazae will make 2-3 nigiri. The "horns" on the shell grow longer where currents flow faster, and are shorter in calmer waters. Some say short-horned sazae taste better when caught on stormy days, but there seems to be little difference in flavor. Remove the operculum "trapdoor," take from shell and cut into flesh, adductor, and liver. Rub salt into flesh and rinse to remove slime and dirt. Never overwash sazae as it damages the flavor. The trick to making sazae into nigiri is to open outwards and score for a crisper bite. Brush with nikiri sauce and add a squeeze of tart sudachi to accentuate the shellfish's own sweetness. Sazae also makes excellent sashimi, and the liver and adductor can be returned to the shell and grilled for a delectable snack. Sazae liver is often bitter, but those I source are sweet and mellow, with flavor to rival the liver of abalone.

horned turban shell

光物 hikarimono (silver-skinned fish)

小肌
(kohada)

小肌は江戸前鮨になくてはならない魚だ。小肌を出せないなら暖簾は上げられないとさえ思うほどである。新子の時季から一年中仕入れは絶やさないが、旬と言えるのは秋の終わりから冬にかけて。特に暮れの頃は脂が乗り、身もふっくらとして最も旨い。産地は、佐賀、熊本・天草、東京湾、三河湾が中心。選ぶのは持ったときにしっかり張りのあるもの。銀の鱗がきれいにつき、腹が裂けていないことも肝心だ。サイズは半身で1貫握れる10cm前後を買うようにしている。仕入れた小肌をいかに〆るか。そこには店の技量や考え方が如実に表れる。念頭に置くのは、江戸前らしいいなせな味。キリッと酢が立つ強めの〆加減に仕立てている。捌く際は1時間ほど氷を入れた塩水に浮かすと鱗が剥がれやすく、皮の模様を傷つけずに済む。2枚におろしたら先に塩で〆、酢洗いをした後に赤酢で本漬けと呼ばれる酢〆をする。〆る時間は身の厚みや気温と湿度で変わり、経験と勘が頼りだ。若い頃、時間をメモしたら親方にこっぴどく怒られたことがある。握りにするのは翌日以降。塩と酢で旨みと香りを引き出した小肌は、鮨のためにある魚と言っても過言ではない。

Kohada is an Edomae sushi stalwart, to the extent that I don't feel right opening up shop unless I can serve it. Though used year-round, right from the first fry, it is tastiest from late autumn to winter. Choose fish that are firm of flesh. Avoid any patchiness in the silvery scales, or tears in the belly. I buy kohada around 10cm long, using half for each piece of nigiri. How the fish is cured is a good indicator of a restaurant's skill and philosophy. First and foremost, it should have a snappy, typically Edomae flavor. I use a strongish marinade for a sharp vinegary tang. To dress kohada, float in iced saltwater for an hour or so to make the fish easier to scale without damaging the skin pattern. Fillet into two pieces, cure with salt, then rinse with vinegar, and use red vinegar for the main marinade. Curing time will depend on the thickness of the flesh, air temperature and humidity; experience and intuition are your guides here. I was reprimanded severely as a novice for noting the time. Use for nigiri from the next day onward. It would be no exaggeration to describe kohada, its umami and fragrance coaxed out by salt and vinegar, as a fish made for sushi.

gizzard shad

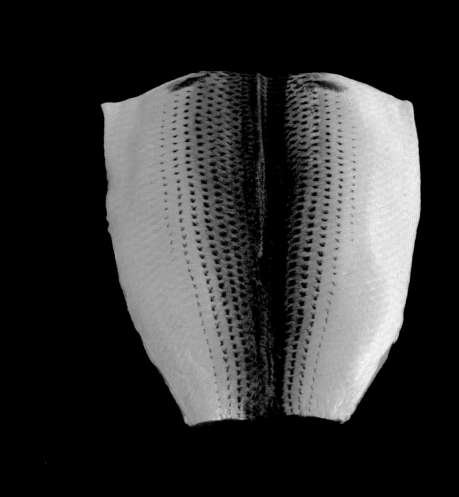

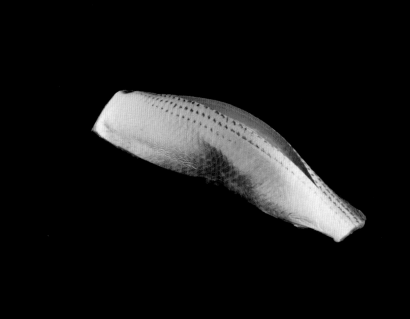

新子
(shinko)

小肌は成長に連れて呼び名が替わる出世魚だ。成魚はコノシロ、逆に小肌より小さい生まれたての稚魚を新子と呼ぶ。市場に並ぶのは夏。時季は年々早まり、昨今は6月下旬から登場する。最初に入荷するのが静岡・舞阪。その後、熊本・天草、愛知・三河、石川、千葉・船橋と続く。入荷初日は鮨屋が競って買い、値段は小肌の十数倍にも跳ね上がる。それを小肌と同じ値段で出すのが鮨屋の意地であり、粋な心意気と修業先で教えられた。新子の到来は鮨屋の元旦でもある。塩と酢の〆加減は初日の新子を基準にしながら、成長に従い日々変えていく。その軸がないと、脂が乗った暮れの小肌の塩梅もブレやすい。「1年の計は新子にあり」というわけだ。買うときに大切なのは腹の裂けがないことと、〆加減を均一にするため極力サイズを揃えること。デリケートな魚のため、仕入れ帰りの車ではエアコンが当たる場所に置き、氷水で手を冷やしながら仕込むのも鉄則だ。小さな新子は数枚で1貫を握り、最近は枚数でお客の気を引く風潮もある。しかし、味のピークは1枚で1貫を握れる8月半ば。軽やかさと小肌の滋味を併せ持ち、これぞ新子と膝打つ旨さだ。

Kohada become konoshiro as adults, and as tiny new fry are shinko. Shinko appear in summer, earlier every year and most recently in late June. On the first day sushi chefs compete to acquire the little fish, paying over ten times the price of kohada. During training I was taught that serving shinko for the same price as kohada showed a sushi chef's honor and pure devotion to his craft. The arrival of shinko also marks the start of a new year for sushi restaurants. Proportions of salt and vinegar are tweaked as the fish grow, using the first day as a baseline, otherwise it is easy to lose track of the correct saltiness for the late, fat-suffused kohada. When buying, check for any tears in the belly, and choose specimens of the same size for uniform curing. On the way home keep these delicate fish near the car's aircon, and cool hands with ice water to prep. With small shinko, several are used for a single nigiri, and lately the fashion has been to dazzle customers by stacking up the fish. Flavor however peaks in August, when a single fish will suffice. Offering both lightness and the richness of kohada, this is when shinko truly comes into its own.

gizzard shad fry

春子
(kasugo)

春子は手のひらほどの小さな鯛。真鯛、黄鯛、血鯛の幼魚の総称で、関西ではこれらに黄鰭の幼魚を加えることもある。産地をずらしながら一年中使うことができるが、関東では春の魚に括られ、関西では秋の魚の一つとされている。東西で旬の捉え方が異なる珍しい魚と言えるだろう。江戸前の鮨屋の間ではその呼び名とともに、桜色をした可憐な皮目の色から春先の鮨ネタというイメージが定着している。小肌同様、塩と酢で〆ることによって味わいが増す魚の代表格であり、白身でなく光物に分類されている。仕入れる産地は和歌山、相模湾、千葉の外房と内房と広範囲にわたり、そのなかから腹がピンと張ったものを選ぶ。〆具合にばらつきが出ないようサイズを揃えることも大切だ。身が柔らかいので、よく切れる包丁で丁寧に捌く。〆加減は小肌よりゆるめにし、フレッシュ感を残すと持ち味を生かせる。ちなみに、古くからの江戸前の仕事には、強く〆てから甘いおぼろをかませる握りもある。ただし、最近はすっきりした風合いが好まれるため、味醂で甘めに加減した酢で〆たり、昆布〆にしたりとその時々で味わいを変えて握ることが多い。

Kasugo are the tiny, palm-sized young of madai, kidai, and chidai species of sea bream, plus, in Kansai, kihada (yellowfin tuna). Though available year-round from different areas, in Kantō they are deemed a spring fish, and in Kansai, an autumn one, in a rare instance of differing views on seafood seasonality. Among Edomae sushi chefs, there is a well-established image of kasugo as a topping for early spring, not only due to its name (literally "child of spring"), but also its lovely cherry blossom-pink skin. Like kohada, kasugo is a typical example of a fish that gains flavor with salt-and-vinegar curing, and is classed not as white fish but hikarimono (silver-skinned fish). Choose specimens with a firm belly, and of the same size, to avoid variations in curing. The flesh is soft, so fillet carefully with a sharp knife. Cure more lightly than kohada to retain a fresh feel and highlight the natural flavor. Edomae tradition includes nigiri topped with well-cured kasugo minced into sweet "oboro," but these days a cleaner texture is preferred, so chefs tweak flavor to suit the occasion, perhaps curing with mirin-sweetened vinegar, or kombu, before making into nigiri.

sea bream fry

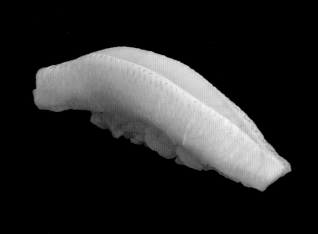

白鱚
(shirokisu)

銀を帯びた色合いが美しい白鱚は白身魚の一種。ただし、鮨屋では光物に入る。江戸前の典型的な鮨ネタだ。旬は4月から9月頃まで。メインで使うのは千葉県・富津と静岡県・舞阪。とりわけ舞阪産は品質がよい。仕入れでは触ると硬く感じるほど身がしっかりし、光沢のあるものを選ぶ。腹に破裂がないことも肝心だ。開いて1尾を揚げる天婦羅では小さいものが好まれるが、鮨は半身で1貫握るため20cmほどの大きなものが向く。仕込みはいささか厄介だ。鱗が多いため盛大に流しが汚れ、〆物なのでその分の手間もかかる。〆方は2通りあり、一つは三枚におろした後、小肌と同じく塩と酢でしっかり〆る方法。もう一つは軽く〆てから皮をさっと湯引きし、身のほうを昆布〆にする方法。キリッとした味を好む方には前者、優しい味を好む方なら後者と使い分けている。余談だが、春の早い時季はたまにヨード臭がすることがある。食べて初めて気づくので、味見が欠かせない魚でもある。最近は握る鮨屋が少なくなっているが、柔らかな口当たりと優しい甘みは白鱚ならでは。皮目に包丁を入れて握ると山葵の鶯色がほんのり透け、見惚れるほどの気品が漂う。

Silvery shirokisu are a white fish species, but in sushi are classed as hikarimono. A classic Edomae topping, in season from April to about September. Choose shiny specimens with flesh very taut to the touch, avoiding any with tears in the belly. Smaller fish are preferred for splaying and cooking whole as tempura, but for sushi those of about 20cm are best, as each half will make one piece of nigiri. Shirokisu can be a hassle to prepare: they have a lot of scales so your sink will get splendidly dirty; and are cured: also time-consuming. There are two approaches to curing. One is to fillet sanmai-oroshi style and firm with salt and vinegar like kohada. The other is to cure lightly then scald the skin quickly, and make kombu-jime with the flesh. For a sharper flavor use the former, and a milder, the latter. In early spring always taste-test, as shirokisu can carry a whiff of iodine only detected on consumption. Though served less by sushi chefs recently, shirokisu has a tender mouthfeel and subtle sweetness all its own. Score skin before making into nigiri, and the green of the wasabi will take on a translucent glow, giving the sushi a captivating air of refinement.

Japanese whiting

真鯖
(masaba)

市場では通年見かける魚だが、ベストシーズンは秋の彼岸から春の彼岸まで。仕入れる産地は神奈川県・松輪、宮城県・金華山沖、兵庫県・淡路、長崎。これらの産地は餌の豊富な海域に棲む根付きの鯖が中心で、釣り物も多い。手釣りの鯖は高値がつくため扱いも丁寧になり、品質のよいものが手に入りやすい。選び方は大型ほどよく1kg以上が理想。ずんぐり太って腹部に張りがあるかを確認する。皮目が黄ばんでいないこともポイントだ。腹を押さえ未消化物があるようなら、身肉の味に影響するので避けたほうがよいだろう。塩と酢で〆るのが定番だが、鮮度が落ちやすいため買ってきたら真っ先に仕込みに取り掛かる。身が割れやすいので、手際よく捌くことが肝心だ。父の世代は鮮度の面から強く〆ていたが、流通が発達した現在は生に近い〆加減でも出せるようになった。その際、20〜30分の時差をつけ、塩〆を長く、酢〆は短めにするのが鉄則だ。脂が十分に乗った最盛期の鯖は、身も柔らかくなめらかだ。程よい塩梅で〆れば濃い旨みを放ちながら、口の中でしなやかにとろけていく。奥深く力強い味わいは鮪に匹敵すると感じるほどだ。

Masaba is in markets year-round, but best from the autumnal to vernal equinox. Mackerel hand-fished in Matsuwa, Kanagawa; off Kinkasan in Miyagi, Awaji in Hyōgo, or Nagasaki fetch top prices so are handled with care, making quality fish easier to obtain. Ideally select fairly big specimens over 1kg, checking that they are sturdy with a firm underbelly, and no yellowing of the skin. Press the belly, and avoid if there is any hint of undigested feed there, as it will affect the flavor of the flesh. Traditionally cured with salt and vinegar, masaba deteriorates quickly, so start prepping as soon as you buy it. The flesh also disintegrates easily, so needs to be handled skillfully. From a freshness perspective chefs of my father's generation used to cure masaba intensely, but today's improved transport allows it to be served in a state close to raw. When doing so, the rule is to do a lengthy salt-cure, and short vinegaring, with 20-30 minutes in between. Mackerel in its oily, succulent prime is also tender and smooth, and cured to just the right degree will melt in the mouth beautifully with intense umami, its robust depth of flavor rivaling that of tuna.

chub mackerel

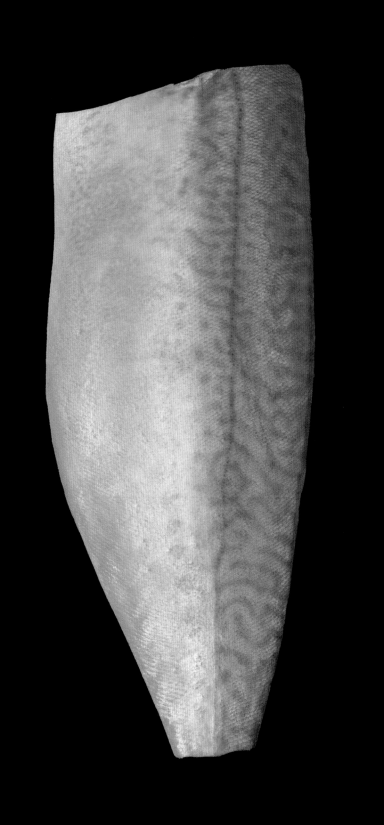

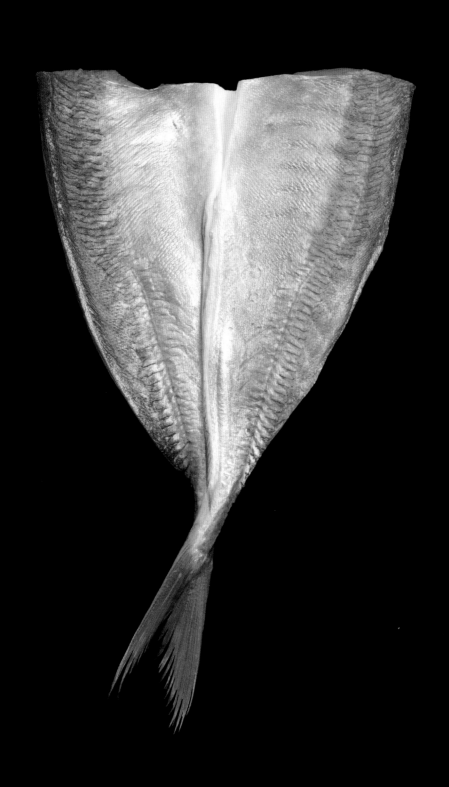

真鯵
(ma-aji)

一年中流通する魚だが、旬は梅雨の時季。産卵に向け栄養を蓄えた真鯵は、丸々太り脂の乗りもピークを迎える。そのなかでも感心するほど旨いのはわずか10日間ほど。身は弾力を保ちながらもすーっと溶け、澄んだ脂の甘みと光物特有の香りを堪能できる。産地は日本全国に分布するが、仕入れるのは九州から千葉まで。船上で活け締めした一本釣りのものから選んでいる。まず見るのは背の色。青や緑がかったものは深いところを泳いでいるため臭みがない。次に見るのは鰓の辺りの張り具合。厚みがあるほど脂の乗りもよい。サイズは半身で1貫握れるほどの大きさがベストだ。頭側と尻尾側では味わいは異なり、半身で握ればそっくり楽しめる。仕込みについては、昔は塩と酢で〆ていたが、流通が発達した現在は〆ずに握る。とはいえ、塩を打ってから酢水で洗い、水分とアクを抜く工程は欠かせない。握る前に小気味よい音を立てて皮を剥ぎ、包丁目を入れて香りを立たせつつ血合いの鮮やかさを見せるのは演出の一つ。薬味は生姜に叩いた青ねぎを合わせ、魚と酢飯の間に挟むことが多い。

Ma-aji are available all year but best in the rainy season, stuffed with nutrients and fat for spawning. Even then they are only tasty enough to be of interest for about ten days, when their flesh is firm but meltingly delicious, with clear, sweet fat, and a distinctive hikarimono aroma. I choose fish caught by pole and line anywhere between Kyūshū and Chiba, and dispatched ikejime-style onboard. Start by studying the color of the back. Fish with a blue or green tinge have been deep swimmers, so will not have any odor. Next look for firmness around the gills: the plumper this area, the more fat on the fish. The optimum size of fish will give two pieces of nigiri. Flavor differs between head and tail, so with a half-fish, you can enjoy both. Though no longer usually cured with salt and vinegar, don't forget to salt and rinse with diluted vinegar to remove excess moisture and "fishiness." Add a performative element by skinning the fish with a satisfying rip, then making a cut with the knife to display the vibrantly colored chiai near the spine, simultaneously releasing the fish's tempting aroma. Often seasoned with ginger and spring onion between the fish and vinegared rice.

Japanese jack mackerel

細魚
(sayori)

真一文字のシャープな体躯と赤い嘴を持つ細魚は、コリッとした歯応え
と、鯵を淡くしたようなすっきりした甘みが持ち味。旬は晩秋から春先ま
でだが、脂が最も乗った12月から1月頃までの細魚を使うことが多い。
仕入れるのは千葉・房州、岩手・三陸、兵庫・淡路で水揚げされた
大型の"閂"だ。閂とは閉じた門扉を固定する横木のことだが、体長
30㎝を超える大物はまさに閂を彷彿とさせるほど太い。身はふっくら
厚く味も乗り、一段上の旨さが楽しめる。この閂のなかでも青光りする
背側の色が鮮やかで、腹にしっかり張りがあるものを選んで買う。細魚
のもう一つの特徴は"腹黒さ"だ。開くと腹の内側が黒い幕でびっし
り覆われている。腹黒い人を「細魚」と呼び替える鮨屋の隠語もある
ほどだ。内臓には錆びた鉄のような強烈な匂いがあり、鮮度がよいほ
どその匂いが強い。これらを塩水で丁寧に洗い落としたら、2枚に開い
て軽く塩をあてて旨みを凝縮させる。かつては酢〆が定番だったが、
新鮮な細魚が手に入る現在はそのまま握ることがほとんど。くるりと丸
めて蕨をかたどった蕨づくりにすると、初春にふさわしい1貫になる。

Sleek in physique, red in beak, crisp to the bite and with a clean sweetness
reminiscent of aji (horse mackerel) but fainter, sayori is in season from late
autumn to early spring. I prefer to use it during December-January when
it carries most fat, choosing larger fish that at over 30cm in length, are
said to resemble the wooden bolt (kannuki) on a traditional gate,
including in girth, and are plump, delectable, and a cut above in umami.
Choose those vibrantly glistening blue on the back, with a firm belly. A
distinctive feature of sayori is its "black-heartedness," in Japanese
literally its "black-bellyness" referring to the black membrane that
covers its insides. In sushi-pro argot, the word sayori is even used to
describe a wicked person. The viscera have an intense, rusty odor,
strongest in the freshest fish. Rinse thoroughly with saltwater to expunge
the membrane, cut the fish open into two pieces and salt lightly to
concentrate the umami. Vinegaring used to be standard, but these days
easier access to fresh sayori means most are made into nigiri without this
curing. Roll up like a fern tip to make a piece of sushi ideal for early spring.

Japanese halfbeak

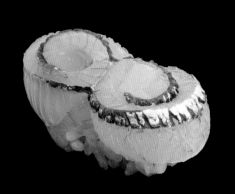

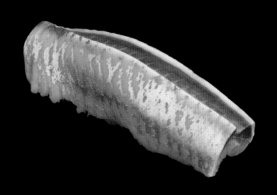

真鰯
(maiwashi)

光物のなかでも鯖に次ぐ脂の強さがある。身と皮の間に白い脂の層があり、ここに旨みが凝縮されている。鰯を餌にする魚は多いが、これを食べるから旨くなるのかと納得する味わいだ。旬は3月から10月だが、"梅雨鰯"という言葉があるように梅雨時は味の深さがピークになる。仕入れる産地は東京湾、千葉の外房と内房、北海道の長万部、大阪湾。11cm以上の中羽や16cm以上の大羽から、腹の裂けがなく目の周りが赤くなっていないものを選ぶ。鱗が剥がれていたり、柄が鮮明でないものもあるが、鰯の場合、脂の乗りを示すので好んで買う。また、背に星のない"ノホシ"も稀にあり、脂の豊かさは驚くほどだ。仕込みで注意すべきは温度管理である。たっぷりの脂は酸化しやすいのが弱点。頭を落とし内臓を出して塩水で洗ったら、そのまま冷蔵庫の一番冷えるところに保存する。開くのは握る直前。そのぐらい気を遣わなければすぐに酸化してしまうのである。それでも自信を持って出せるのは夕方6時までが限界だ。これ以降に握る場合は、塩と酢で〆るようにしている。鰯に合うのは山葵よりも生姜。すっきりとした辛味が脂の甘みを爽やかに引き立てる。

Sardines have an unapologetic fattiness second only to mackerel among the hikarimono or "silver-skinned fish," the layer of white fat between skin and flesh concealing a concentrated blast of umami. Sardines are in season from March to October, but have greatest depth of flavor during the rainy season (June-July). Choose medium-sized specimens over 11cm (chūba), or large over 16cm (ōba), with no tears in the belly or red around the eyes. Missing scales or lack of a clear pattern are indicators of subcutaneous fat, and thus positives in sardines. Very occasionally you will spot sardines without stars on the back, and these have amazing amount of fat. When it comes to preparation, temperature control is key. A demerit of sardines is the rapidity with which their ample fat can oxidize. Remove heads, gut, rinse in saltwater, then transfer immediately to the coldest part of the fridge. Only split open when ready to make into nigiri, or the fat will oxidize. Even with these precautions, I am only confident serving sardines to 6pm. After that it's a matter of curing with salt and vinegar. Ginger is better than wasabi on sardine nigiri, its bracing bite accentuating the fish's sweetness.

sardine

海老 ebi (shrimp/prawn)

車海老
(kuruma-ebi)

　"才巻""巻"とサイズで呼び名が変わり、鮨屋が使うのは20cm近い"車"とさらに大きい"大車"。大きいほど香りが強く甘みも濃い。1年中用意するネタだが、味が乗るのは秋の終わりから冬にかけて。愛知・三河、熊本・天草、神奈川・横須賀沖が名産地として知られ、わずかに羽田沖も入る。どの産地も天然の活け物が絶対条件だ。目がよく動けば生きがよく、ヒゲの有無も管理の見極めになる。持ち味を生かすには生ではなく茹でるに限る。おめでたい紅白模様が浮き出て、歯切れのよい弾力と瑞々しい甘みが堪能できる。茹で方も重要だ。欠かせないのは沸騰させて一晩置いた湯冷まし。酸素を抜いた重たい水で茹でると色気が出ると教わった。茹で時間は沸いた湯に入れた海老がふっと動いた瞬間から1分20秒。「動く瞬間」の見極めが肝心である。茹で上がったら殻をむき腹を開いて背わたを除いた後、軽く塩で〆る。ここまでを握る20分前に行なってピークで出す。シャリも別に保温し温度を合わせ、香りが強ければ山葵をすり直す。食べやすいよう尾を取る店もあるが、扇形の尾は末広がりの縁起物のため、残して華のある姿に握るのが流儀だ。

These prawns have different names according to size: saimaki, maki, kuruma and ōguruma, and sushi chefs use kuruma-ebi, close to 20cm long, and the even larger ōguruma. The bigger the prawn, the sweeter the flesh and more intoxicating the fragrance. A year-round topping, they are best from late autumn into winter. Source live: fast-moving eyes indicate vitality. The presence or lack of whiskers will affect how you prepare them. To optimize their natural flavor, prawns must be boiled, coloring them an auspicious red and white, and adding a pleasing resilience and zingy sweetness. The boiling method is also crucial. Bring water to the boil, then leave overnight to cool. I was taught that prawns boiled in the resulting "heavy" water with less oxygen will be a better color. Boil for 1 minute 20 seconds from the time the prawn twitches on being placed in the boiling water. Identifying this precise moment is vital. When boiled, peel, split, devein and salt lightly. Do all this 20 minutes before making into nigiri to serve prawns at their peak. Conventionally kuruma-ebi retains its attractive fan-shaped tail as a symbol of prosperity, though some restaurants remove it for easier eating.

Japanese tiger prawn

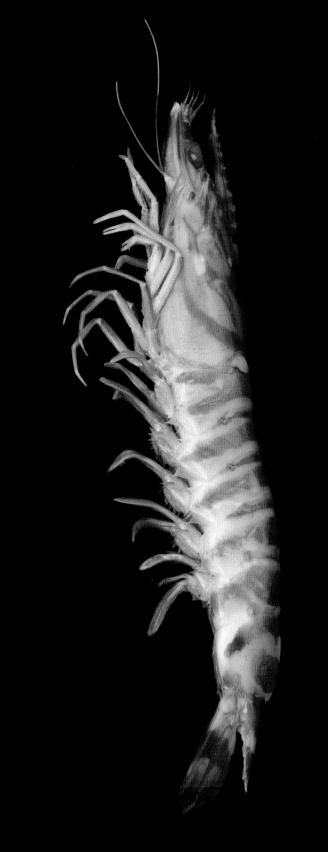

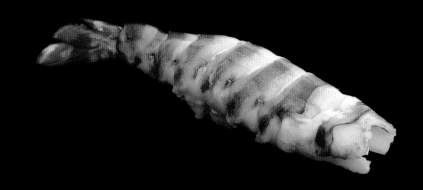

牡丹海老
(botan-ebi)

茹でて握る車海老に対して、生のままで持ち味が映えるのが牡丹海老である。ただし、牡丹海老自体は非常に希少で、流通する多くは正確には"富山海老"という種類になる。両者は見た目がわずかに違い、富山海老は明るい朱色の殻に褐色の横縞があり、ノコギリ状の頭部に白い斑紋が散らばる。体長20㎝前後になる大型種でもある。旬は12月から4月までと比較的長い。産地の中でも京都・丹後や北海道・噴火湾が名高く、このうちよく使うのは後者の噴火湾産だ。上品で澄んだ甘みがあり、ぷりぷりと弾むような舌触りが堪能できる。また、噴火湾をはじめ北海道産は総じて流通の状態がよく、鮮度の面も秀でている。買うときは殻に透明感があり、白い斑紋がはっきりしているものを見繕う。透けて見える頭の味噌が黒ずんでいないこともポイントだ。握りにする場合は、殻を向いて軽く塩を当て水分を抜くと、甘みがクリアになってシャリとの馴染みもよくなる。特に海老好きには喜ばれるネタだ。あるいは、昆布〆にして先付として出すこともある。昆布で〆ると口当たりがねっとりと艶かしくなり、旨みも凝縮されるので酒を呼ぶ一品になる。

Kuruma-ebi is boiled before use in nigiri, but botan-ebi is most delectable raw. Genuine botan-ebi are extremely rare, and most at market actually belong to a species known as "Toyama ebi." Very similar in appearance, Toyama ebi has a vibrant scarlet shell and brown horizontal stripes, with a scattering of white spots on a saw-toothed head, and is a large shrimp, around 20 cm. The season is relatively long, lasting from December to April. Renowned sources are Tango in Kyōto and Funka (Uchiura) Bay in Hokkaidō; I use ebi from the latter due to its refined, unadulterated sweetness and zingy mouthfeel. Hokkaidō shrimps also generally ship faster, and are thus fresher. Buy shrimp with translucent shells and obvious spotting. Also check that the brain matter in the see-through head has not turned black. For nigiri, shell and salt lightly to remove moisture for a clarified sweetness that is also a better match with sushi rice. Alternatively, cure with kombu and serve as an appetizer. Kombu curing gives the shrimps an irresistibly moist texture and concentrated umami that go wonderfully with a drink.

botan shrimp

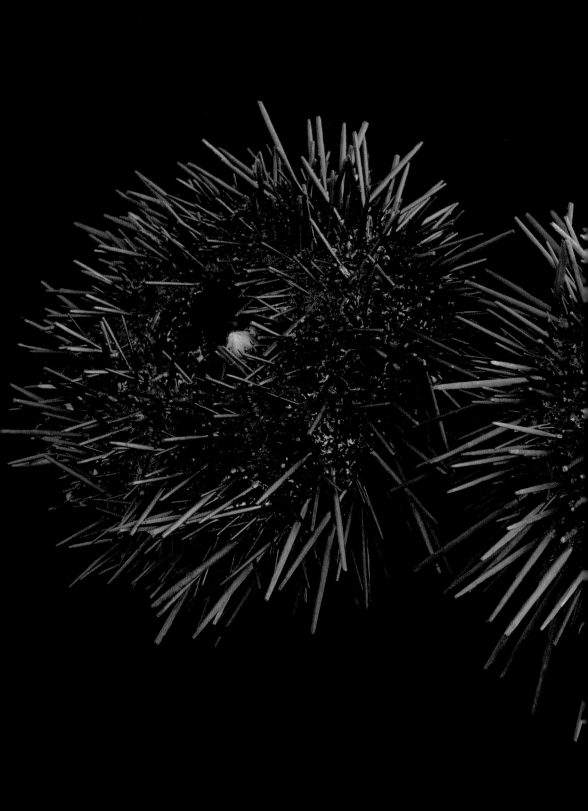

魚卵 gyoran (roe)

雲丹
(uni)

一年を通じて各地からさまざまな種類が市場に並ぶ。ざっくり季節を辿ると、1月から8月にかけては北海道の羅臼や日高で獲れた馬糞雲丹、秋口から12月には同じく北海道の松前や利尻から紫雲丹が到来。7月中旬から8月中旬には熊本・天草や佐賀の赤雲丹も登場する。店で使うのは主に北海道産で、馬糞雲丹の人気が高い。紫雲丹がクリーミーで軽い甘みなのに対し、馬糞雲丹は旨みが濃く純粋な甘みが楽しめるからだろう。赤雲丹は良品が入ったとき手がのびる。見映えはしないが、磯の香りを含んだ独特の甘みが持ち味だ。仕入れの極意は仲買人と信頼関係を築き、薦められた品を買う。これに尽きる。雲丹に限っては見た目で判断できず、水産会社のブランドも味に直結するとは限らない。信頼を得るには日頃から値段を気にせずに買うこと。するとよいものが自然と回ってくる。雲丹といえば軍艦巻きの印象が強いが、シャリだけで握ることもある。海苔に負けない香りがあれば軍艦巻きにするなどケースバイケースだ。雲丹のように崩れやすい握りを手綱（手渡し）する店もあるが、どんなネタでも箸で持てるよう握るのが職人の仕事だと考える。

Uni is available all year round, from different locations. From January into early August, Hokkaidō bafun uni caught in the likes of Rausu and Hidaka arrive, then from early autumn to December, murasaki uni from Matsumae and Rishiri, also in Hokkaidō, and from mid-July to mid-August, aka-uni from Amakusa in Kumamoto, and Saga. I mainly use Hokkaidō uni, with bafun especially popular. While murasaki uni are creamy and only subtly sweet, bafun uni offer a more intense umami and unalloyed sweetness. Aka-uni I will use if good quality specimens come in; though not as visually attractive, it has a distinctive briny succulence of its own. Obtaining the best uni involves building a good relationship with your supplier, and buying what they suggest. Appearance and brand have no bearing on flavor: buy regardless of price, and the best uni will be yours. Uni is often associated with gunkan-maki, but I also combine it just with rice. If the uni has a fragrance to rival the nori, for example, I may use it in gunkan-maki. Some restaurants serve fragile nigiri like uni hand to hand, but in my view it is the chef's job to ensure that a nigiri with any topping can be held with chopsticks.

sea urchin

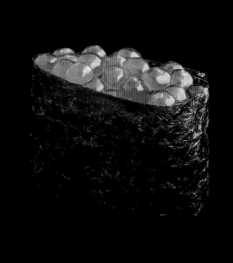

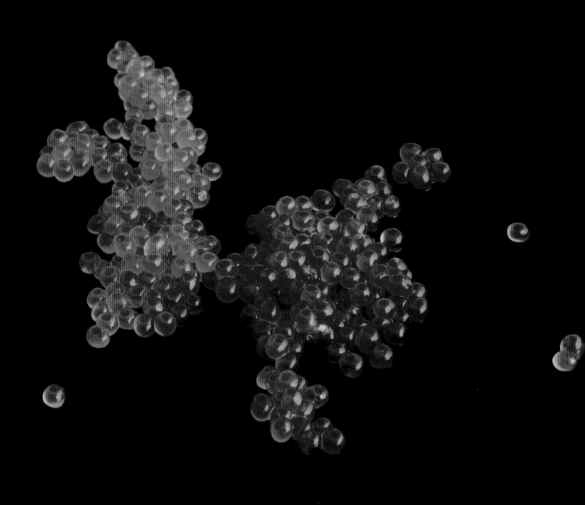

イクラ

(ikura)

川で生まれた鮭は大海を泳いで成長したのち、再び、故郷の川に戻って産卵をする。遡上前の鮭は無数の卵を腹に蓄えはち切れんばかりだ。この卵は筋子と呼ばれ、ほぐして味付けすればイクラとなる。筋子の最盛期は夏の終わりから11月頃まで。市場にはアラスカ産も出回るが、仕入れるのはもっぱら北海道産、なかでも9月頃に道東沖で水揚げされたものがベストだ。出始めの筋子は皮が薄く柔らかく、とろけるような口当たりのイクラができる。仕込み方はさまざまだが、店では熱湯で卵をほぐす。生の筋子に沸きたての湯を一気に注ぐと、卵を覆う膜が縮んでするっと面白いようにほぐれる。同時に、薄皮が落ちるので、舌触りが一層なめらかになる。もちろん、熱湯を注いだ後の手際も大切だ。熱が入らないうちに水を注ぎ、その後も幾度となく水洗いを繰り返し、これ以上きれいにならないところでざるに上げる。このときは白く靄がかかっているが、ひと掴みの塩を加えるとルビー色へと戻るから面白い。イクラの握りは軍艦巻きが定番だ。江戸前伝統のネタではないが、漆黒の海苔と真紅のイクラのコンビネーションは見映えという点でも絶妙である。

Salmon born in rivers and growing up at sea return to their birthplace to spawn, bellies crammed with roe before they head upstream. Known as sujiko, and tastiest from late summer to November, once separated and seasoned this roe becomes ikura. Alaskan sujiko is available, but I use exclusively Hokkaidō roe, especially from fish landed off the east coast around September. Early sujiko has a soft, thin membrane, and makes melt-in-the-mouth ikura. There are various ways to prepare ikura, but I use boiling water to separate the eggs. Pour just-boiled water in one go over sujiko to shrink the covering sac, separating the roe with surprising smoothness. This will also remove the thin film around the individual eggs, giving them a sleeker mouthfeel. Pour over cold water quickly before the roe cooks from the heat, then rinse repeatedly, and drain when you are happy with how it looks. By now the roe will have a white haze, but adding a pinch of salt will magically restore its lovely ruby red. Ikura nigiri is a gunkan-maki classic, and though not a traditional Edomae topping, the combination of shiny black nori and vermilion roe is hard to beat for beauty.

salmon roe

鱈子
(tarako)

お任せの握りは来店する方の好みを踏まえて構成する。苦手なネタがあれば代わりになるものを考え、同席者と同じ数の握りを出して満足して帰っていただくのが鮨屋の務めだ。鱈子の握りは生の魚を得意としない方がいらしたとき、苦肉の策として思いついた鮨ネタである。ヒントをもらったのは小田原でふらりと入った鮨屋。そこではいくらの代わりに鱈子を握り、シャリとの意外な相性に感心したものだ。もちろん、店で出すからにはどんな鱈子でもよいわけではない。使うのは名産地の北海道・虎杖浜産。その中でも皇室献上品になる特級の品を仕入れている。初めて見たときには大きさと見事な艶に圧倒された。まさに桁違いである。口にするとさらりとなめらかにほぐれ、大きな粒がぷちぷちと弾ける。味わいにも気品があり、塩の塩梅も絶妙だ。漬け地の材料には天然塩などが選りすぐられ、着色料は使わず自然の色合いが生かされている。山葵は入れず、粒が見えるように握ると見映えのする1貫になる。邪道ではあるが、召し上がった方は「こんなファンタスティックな鮨は初めて」と大絶賛。変化球の一つとしてあってもよいのだろう。

My omakase offerings are based on customer preference. If there is a topping someone dislikes, it's the sushi chef's job to think of an alternative so that person leaves content that they have received the same number of nigiri as their companions. Tarako nigiri is my last resort when faced with a customer not keen on raw fish. Obviously, if I'm serving it at the restaurant, it can't be just any old roe: mine comes from Kojōhama in Hokkaidō, famous for tarako, and is the same premium stuff supplied to the imperial household. On first sight I was astounded by the size and sheen of this incomparable royal roe. It falls smoothly apart in the mouth, plump eggs popping. The taste is similarly refined, the salting perfect. Only the finest natural ingredients, including salt, are used for preserving it, and no coloring, thus showcasing the natural color of the roe. Formed into nigiri without wasabi, the individual eggs visible, tarako makes quite an impressive sushi offering. Though not quite "proper," it will be praised by the customer as the most amazing sushi they've ever had. An excellent if slightly offbeat topping to have up one's sleeve.

cod roe

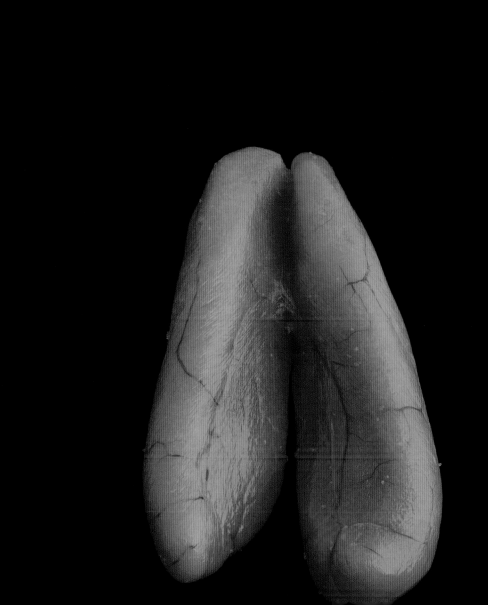

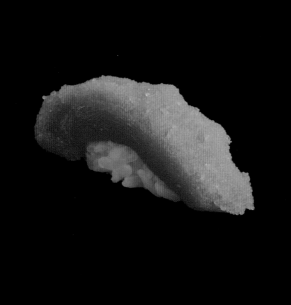

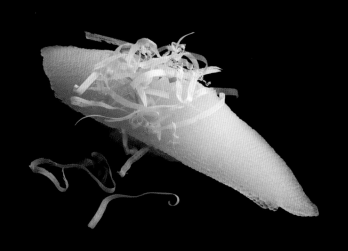

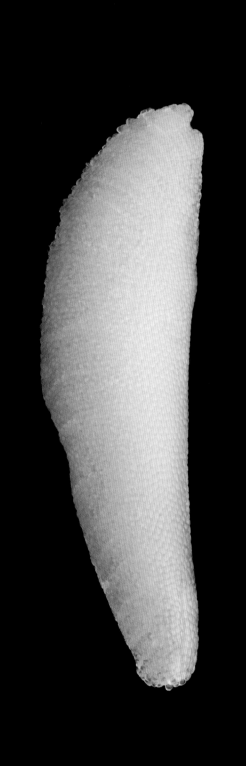

数の子
(kazunoko)

数の子は鰊の卵巣を塩漬け、または乾燥させたもの。子孫繁栄の縁起物として御節料理に欠かせない。市場では一年中売られているが、仕入れたくなるのはやはり年の瀬から年明けにかけてだ。手にすると正月が近づいていることを実感する、季節感に富んだ鮨ネタだ。産地は北海道の留萌のほか、アラスカやロシアからの輸入物も多い。市場に並ぶのは塩蔵が主流で、干した品は入荷が少なく高級品として扱われる。味がよいのも干数の子のため、できる限りこれを買うようにしている。乾燥と塩蔵、どちらについても戻し方にコツがある。用意するのは薄い塩水。ここに数の子を浸けたら、4〜5日かけて少しずつ塩分濃度を緩めていく。塩水は朝晩こまめに替えることも大切だ。全体が十分に戻ったら表面を覆う薄い膜を取り除き、薄味のだし汁に半日ほど浸けて味付けをする。つまみはもちろん、要望があれば握りにもする。シャリと抜群に合うわけではないが、年末年始にふさわしい1貫となる。「数の子は音で食べるもの」とは北大路魯山人の言葉だが、言い得て妙である。パリパリと歯に響く小気味よい音色もまた、季節の風物詩と言えるだろう。

A fertility symbol staple of Japanese New Year's cooking, kazunoko is salted or dried herring roe. Though always available, around New Year festivities is indeed the usual time to buy it in, as a topping strongly associated with this season. Sourced from Rumoi in Hokkaidō, or often imported from Alaska or Russia, most kazunoko on sale is salted, with a small amount of dried product available as a luxury option. Dried kazunoko also tastes better, so is best if available. The trick to successfully rehydrating both salted and dried kazunoko is to prepare some fairly dilute saltwater, add the kazunoko and soak for 4-5 days, gradually reducing the salt concentration and remembering to change the water completely morning and night. When all the roe is sufficiently rehydrated, remove the thin membrane covering the surface, and marinate for half a day in a thin dashi broth for flavor. Though used often in tsumami and not an outstanding match for sushi rice, it is a suitable offering at New Year. Artist and epicure Kitaōji Rosanjin aptly noted that "one eats kazunoko by the sound," and no New Year in Japan is complete without its gratifying crunch.

herring roe

職人の技
waza (techniques)

昆布〆
(kombu-jime)

昆布〆は江戸前鮨に欠かせない仕事の一つである。電気冷蔵庫がな
かった時代に、保存性を高めるために生まれた技法と言われている。
昆布で挟めば魚の水分もほどよく抜け、昆布の旨みを魚に移せる。見
立てよりも魚の味が薄かったときにも役立つ技法だ。使う昆布は羅臼産
の天然物。昆布蔵で2〜3年寝かせ、旨みを凝縮させた品を選んでい
る。柵取りした魚を挟むため、着物の帯ほどの幅が必須である。使う
前には日本酒で表面を拭いて汚れをさっと落とす。このとき旨み成分で
ある白い粉を拭き取らないこと。昆布〆にする魚は鱚、春子、鮃、真鯛、
真子鰈、鰤といった白身や光物が主体だが、鮪や烏賊も意外な旨さが
引き出される。古くなった魚を昆布で〆ても旨くはならないので、鮮度の
よさは必須条件だ。〆方は柵にした魚に軽く塩を打ち、汗をかいたら拭
き取って昆布で挟んでラップをかけるのみ。輪ゴムで固定したり重石を
かけたりすると、水分が抜け過ぎて硬くなる上、魚の味を殺してしまうか
らだ。冷蔵庫の一番冷えないところに入れ、〆る時間は1時間から長く
ても半日。魚の風味と瑞々しさを残すのが昆布〆の要諦といえるだろう。

Kombu-jime is a vital process in Edomae sushi, originally designed in the days
before refrigeration to help fish keep longer. Sandwiching between sheets of
kombu removes just the right amount of moisture and transfers the seaweed's
umami to the fish, making it handy for fish with less flavor than its appearance
suggests. I choose umami-rich kombu aged 2-3 years. A saku block of fish
requires a sheet about the width of a kimono sash. Give the kombu a quick
wipe with sake to clean it, taking care not to remove the white powder that
provides the umami. Kombu curing is mostly used for white-fleshed or silver-
skinned species such as whiting, kasugo, flounder, sea bream, marbled sole,
and barracuda, but also teases a surprising amount of flavor from tuna and
squid. Freshness is all: kombu curing will not make fish that has been sitting
around too long taste better. Just lightly salt fish blocks, wipe off sweat, then
place between kombu sheets and wrap in clingfilm. Avoid rubber bands or
weights, as this will dry the fish too much, making it tough and destroying the
flavor. Place in the warmest part of the fridge for an hour to a half-day at the
most. The point of kombu curing is to retain the flavor and succulence of the fish.

kombu curing

ヅケ

(zuke)

ヅケは江戸前の古典的な仕事の代表だ。保冷の設備がなかった江戸時代、魚の保存法として発達した。浸け地は醤油、酒、味醂でつくった煮切り醤油。一般的なのは柵で浸け込む方法だ。熱湯にくぐらせ湯霜にしてから煮切り醤油に入れ、30分おきに向きを変えながら浸けること約1時間。水分がほどよく抜け、内側がねっとりと熟れていく。香りには熟成香が生まれ、旨みは凝縮されて深くなる。ヅケにして旨い魚の代表は鮪の赤身だ。特に背骨に近いテンパ（天端）と呼ばれる部分は血の気が多く香りも強いため、煮切り醤油に浸けても鮪の味がしっかり感じられてバランスが絶妙だ。鮪ではトロもいい。濃厚ながらさっぱりとして、とろける口当たりが楽しめる。真梶木もヅケにして映える魚だ。淡白さが補われ、もっちり艶っぽい味わいになる。一方、ヅケには切りつけしてから軽く浸ける方法もあり、鰤にはこれを用いている。表面の脂が落ち、軽やかな味わいになる。思えば、ヅケは鮮度第一だった高度成長期に、過去の遺物と葬られた技。しかし、昨今は江戸前の古い仕事を好んで取り入れる鮨屋が増えている。温故知新とはこれをいうのだろう。

A classic Edomae technique, zuke developed as a means of fish preservation in the pre-refrigeration days of the Edo period. Fish is usually marinated in saku blocks in a nikiri sauce made from shōyu, sake, and mirin. Scald fish with boiling water and steep in nikiri sauce for an hour or so, turning after 30 minutes. This will remove the right amount of moisture, and mature the inside into sticky succulence. The fish takes on an aged aroma, while umami becomes condensed, with added depth. Tuna akami is the pre-eminent example of fish that is a revelation when marinated. In particular, the part known as tenpa near the backbone is bloody and aromatic, so retains solid tuna taste even after zuke, creating an exquisite flavor balance. Striped marlin is another fish that truly takes to zuke, which adds sultry, piquant pep to its subtle flavor. A light zuke after making slashes in the flesh is another option, which I use for amberjack. Fat falls off the surface for a lighter taste. Zuke was dismissed as a relic of the past in Japan's more prosperous years when freshness trumped all, but is enjoying a revival among sushi chefs eager to incorporate something of old Edo in their offerings.

marinating

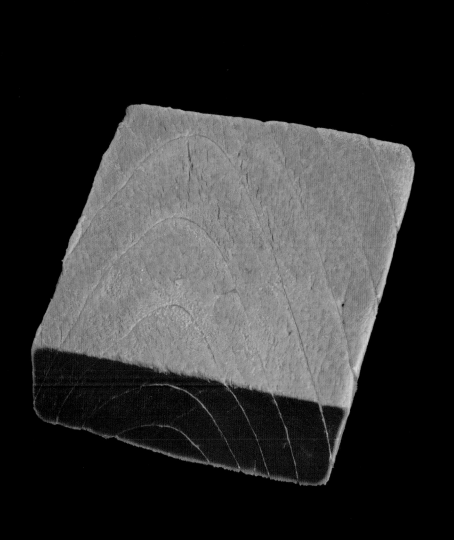

白魚の桜葉蒸し
(shirauo-no-sakurabamushi)

春の気配を感じ始める2月から桜が咲く4月までの、季節を味わう握りである。父や修業先では春先になると必ずこの握りを仕立ていた。使うのはこの時季が旬の白魚。体長5〜10cmほどの楔形をした、海水と真水が混ざる汽水域に生息する魚である。仕入れるのは島根県宍道湖産。汽水域の魚は時折、泥臭さを感じることがあるが、宍道湖産はその心配がなく見た目も美しい。この白魚に春の香りを添えるのが桜の葉の塩漬けだ。二晩かけてしっかりと塩抜きをしたら、白魚を1本ずつ筏状に並べて日本酒を数滴。上にも桜の葉を掛け、蒸し器で3〜5秒ほど湯気に当てたら取り出して冷ます。握るときには上の葉を外し、ひっくり返してシャリと合わせて葉の上から握る。その葉を引くと純白の白魚が現れるという寸法だ。桜の香りをほんのり纏った白魚は柔らかく繊細で、ほろ苦さと淡い甘みがふんわりとほどけ出す。この握りには、山葵に替えておろし生姜をかませるのが定番。すっきりとした辛みが味わいを引き締め、爽やかな余韻を残す。白魚と桜の葉は春の訪れを予感させる、まさに出合い物。冬の寒さを乗り越えたご褒美のような1貫だ。

This nigiri is a taste of the season, served from the first hint of spring in February, to the blossoming of cherry trees in April, and made using the wedge-shaped shirauo 5-10cm long that inhabit brackish waters. Fish from these mixed fresh and saltwater environments can taste muddy, but the shirauo I use from Lake Shinji in Shimane never do, and look good as well. Salted cherry leaves add a whiff of spring. After desalinating thoroughly over two nights, arrange shirauo one at a time on leaves in raft formation and sprinkle over a few drops of sake. Place another leaf on top, steam for 3-5 seconds, remove and cool. To make nigiri, remove the top leaf, flip, and form into nigiri with the rice on the leaf. The idea is for the pure white shirauo to appear when that leaf is taken away. The fish with its cherry hint is tender and delicate, a soft, unraveling parcel of subtle bitterness and airy sweetness. Grated ginger, not wasabi, is the standard accompaniment, its invigorating tang focusing the flavor and leaving a refreshing aftertaste. Shirauo and cherry leaf are the perfect pairing to herald the coming of spring; a reward for making it through the cold of winter.

shirauo steamed in a cherry leaf

筋子
(sujiko)

イクラの項でも書いた通り、生の筋子は夏の終わりから市場に出回り、晩秋の11月頃まで仕入れることができる。日を追うごとに鮭を獲る海域は変わり、遡上する川に近づくほど卵の皮が硬くなる。産卵に向け、卵を丈夫にしたいという本能のなせる業だろう。皮が硬いと口当たりが悪くなるので、10月後半からの生の筋子はほぐさずにそのまま漬け込むことが多い。この場合、生の筋子から血管の黒い筋を取り除くことから仕込みがスタートする。1本1本、ピンセットで取り除くのはなかなか根気のいる作業だ。きれいに掃除したら塩を打ち、程よく水分を抜く。魚同様、旨みを凝縮するためであり、ねっとりとした舌触りも生み出される。この後、塩を落としたら、醤油、酒、味醂に鰹だしを少々加えた漬け地に漬け込めば完成である。早ければ半日、長くても1日で出すことができる。塩漬けした市販の筋子のように塩辛くはせず、そのまま口にできる塩梅に仕上げるのがコツだ。自家製の筋子は磯辺巻きの要領で海苔に包むと酒の肴に絶好だ。イクラもしかりだが、冷凍はしないので出せるのは12月いっぱい。わずかな期間だけ楽しめる季節の味の一つだ。

As noted earlier, raw sujiko appears from the end of summer, and is available until around November. As the days pass, salmon are caught in different locations, the membrane on their eggs toughening as they move toward the river, likely to render the roe more robust ahead of spawning. A hard skin makes for unpleasant eating, so from the second half of October onward raw sujiko is often cured with egg sac intact. In this instance, begin by deveining the sac; a task requiring a set of tweezers and a lot of patience. Then salt to dehydrate somewhat. As with fish, this concentrates umami, and gives a stickier texture. Rinse off salt, then steep in a marinade of shōyu, sake, mirin and a little katsuo dashi stock. The sujiko will be ready to serve in half a day at the earliest, and a full day at the latest. The trick is to finish it in a way that allows it to be eaten as is, without the saltiness of commercial salted sujiko. Wrapped in nori isobemaki-style, homemade sujiko makes a delectable snack with drinks. Like ikura, sujiko is not frozen, so can only be served to the end of December, making it a fleeting seasonal indulgence.

salmon roe skein

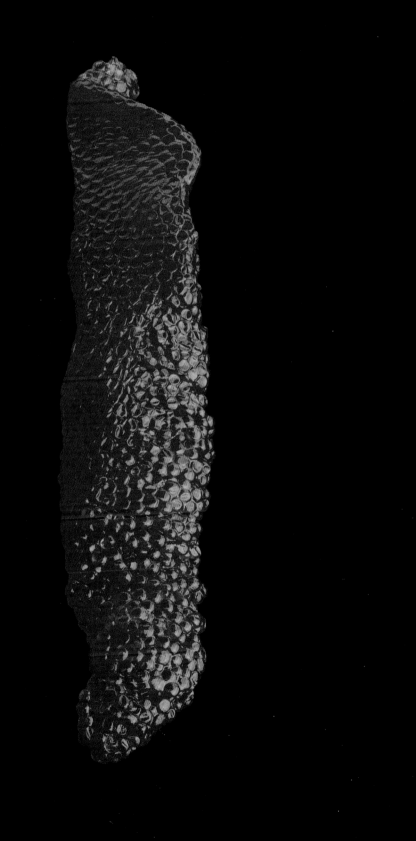

玉子焼
(tamagoyaki)

江戸前の鮨屋の玉子焼は芝海老や白身魚のすり身を入れたカステラ風が定番。修業したどの店でもこのタイプの玉子焼きを出していた。しかし、父が焼いていたのはほんのり甘いだし巻玉子だ。店を構える国分寺ではだし巻のほうが受けがよかったという。暖簾を継いでからは父に倣ってだし巻を出していたが、自分らしい玉子焼はできないものかと考える中で生まれたのが現在の玉子焼である。目指したのは鮨屋の玉子焼とだし巻の中間。生地はだし巻に近いが、焼き方が異なる。強火ではなく、極弱火で薄いクレープ状に広げて20〜22層に巻いていく。食べ心地はたとえて言うならプリン。低温でゆっくり火を入れることで、ぷるんと瑞々しい食感に仕上がる。だしの漉し方にもコツがある。鰹節を煮出したら、水出しコーヒーの要領でゆっくりポタポタと3時間かけて落とす。鰹節の甘みが十二分に引き出され、ほんの少しの砂糖でも甘く焼き上がる。焼くのは決まって開店の3時間前。味が落ち着き、人肌の温度で出せるからだ。そのままつまみたいという注文が多いが、小さなシャリに玉子焼がまたがる鞍掛で握るのが個人的には好みである。

The standard Edomae sushi tamagoyaki resembles spongecake containing shiba-ebi or white fish surimi. Every restaurant I trained at served this type of tamagoyaki. On taking over my father's business, I instead followed his practice of making a dashimaki omelette using stock, but now serve my own version somewhere between the standard sushi chef tamagoyaki, and dashimaki. The mix is close to dashimaki, but the cooking is different. Instead of a hot flame, I spread the mix thin as a crepe on a very low heat, building up 20-22 layers into something resembling a soft pudding in mouthfeel. Cooking slowly at a low temperature gives a moist, springy, finish. There's also a trick to straining the dashi. Once the katsuobushi (bonito flakes) come to the boil, strain at a drip for 3 hours in the manner of cold-brewed coffee. This wrings all the sweetness from the katsuobushi, achieving a sweet omelette with only a smidgeon of sugar. I always cook tamagoyaki three hours before opening; this allows the flavor to take, and lets me serve it at skin temperature. Many order it as is to snack on, but my own preference is to make nigiri with a small amount of rice and the egg placed kurakake (saddle) style on top.

omelette

干瓢巻
(kanpyō-maki)

鮨屋で海苔巻といえば干瓢巻を指す。"鉄砲"という粋な呼び名もあり、江戸前の鮨屋に欠かせない巻物だ。そもそも干瓢とは"瓢"と呼ばれる夕顔の果実を紐状に剥いて乾燥させたもの。使うのは有数の産地である栃木県産。無漂白のものを選ぶようにしている。仕込みは3日がかりだ。初日は長い干瓢を海苔の長さに合わせて切り、塩と水を入れて揉み洗いする。この作業を数回繰り返した後、水を切り、茹でるのは翌日だ。茹で加減は爪がすっと刺さる柔らかさ。コシが抜けるので茹で過ぎは禁物である。茹で上がったら重石をして、再び一晩、水を切る。3日目は醤油、ざらめ、酒で煮汁をつくり、煮汁がなくなるまで煮含める。干瓢には50年以上使い続けている鍋があり、煮汁の痕がつくので量の加減もしやすい。煮上げた干瓢の出番は握りを一通り出し終わってから。「最後に巻物はいかがですか」と伺い、要望があれば簀に海苔とシャリを広げて細巻にする。火を通したものには山葵を入れないのが基本だ。仕込みに手間暇はかかるが、干瓢を切らしたことはない。それほど大事なものであり、店の考え方も表れる物差しといえるだろう。

When a sushi chef says norimaki, they are referring to that Edomae sushi staple kanpyō-maki, also known by the slightly more dashing name "teppō" meaning cannon. Kanpyō is the fruit of calabash cut into strips and dried. I always choose unbleached kanpyō from Tochigi. Preparation takes three days. On the first, cut the long ribbons of kanpyō to match the length of the nori, add salt and water and wash, rubbing as you do. Repeat this process several times, then drain in preparation for boiling the next day. Boil only until soft enough to be easily pierced by a fingernail. Next, place a weight on top and leave one more night to drain. On the third day make a liquor from shōyu, granulated sugar and sake, and simmer kanpyō until reduced completely. This kanpyō makes its appearance when I have more or less finished serving nigiri. I ask if the customer would like makimono to finish, and if so, spread nori and rice on a sushi mat, followed by kanpyō, and roll into a thin hosomaki roll. As a basic rule, don't add wasabi to anything cooked. Though time-consuming to prepare, kanpyō is so important I always have some on hand. It is another measure of the chef's approach to his craft.

dried calabash roll

職人の極意
gokui (top tips)

米
(kome)

鮨の味の6〜7割はシャリで決まる。旨いシャリをつくるには米選びが肝心だ。条件は粘りが少ないこと。握ったときに崩れにくく、口の中でほろりとほどけるのが理想だ。魚の味を後押しする甘みもほしい。甘みのもとはでんぷん質だが、でんぷん質は粘りも生むため、希望通りの米を探すのは容易ではない。仕入れるのは新潟県の魚沼産と栃尾産をブレンドしたコシヒカリ。山間部に田んぼがあり、昼夜の寒暖差から良質の米が採れる。粘りを抑えるため、使うのは温度と水分を管理した前年産の古米だ。秋の新米の時季は古米のみ。その後、季節を追って少しずつ新米を配合し、味と粘りのバランスを保つ。米の選定や配合は新潟「長岡米専」の協力で叶えられている。炊き方も重要だ。力強く研いで糠層を取り、水を張って冷蔵庫に入れる。冷えた状態から炊くと甘みと艶が出るからだ。炊飯には対流のよいガスの羽釜を使い、来店時間の60分前に炊いてシャリ切りすると、温度と酢のまわりがちょうどよくなる。来店が30分遅れたら炊き直すほど気を遣う。シャリ酢は酒粕を主原料にしたコクのある赤酢。これも半年以上寝かせ角を取ることが欠かせない。

Sixty to seventy percent of sushi's flavor is determined by the quality of the vinegared rice known as "shari," so choosing the best rice is imperative. Ideally it should not be too sticky, but remain intact when pressed into nigiri, only disintegrating, smoothly, once in the mouth, its sweetness further enhancing the taste of the fish. This sweetness comes from its starch, which also makes it glutinous, so finding the perfect rice for the job is tricky. I use koshihikari stored from the previous year under temperature- and humidity-controlled conditions. During the new rice season of autumn, old rice is my sole choice. After that, as the seasons progress I gradually blend in a little more new rice to maintain the right balance of flavor and stickiness. The cooking is just as important. Rinse raw grains rigorously to remove surface starch, add water and refrigerate. Cooking from chilled makes for sweet, glossy shari. I find cooking and turning the rice an hour before the customers arrive perfect in terms of both temperature and adding the vinegar. The vinegar for the rice is a robust red variety (akazu) made primarily from sake lees, that also needs to be set aside for at least six months to take the edge off.

rice

海苔
(nori)

海苔は鮨の名脇役である。細巻、太巻、軍艦巻、握りに巻く帯など手にする場面は多い。海苔の選び方でまず大切なのはやはり香りだ。父の時代には茶箱に半年分の海苔を入れて家で保管していたが、その部屋は海苔の香りでむせ返るほどだったことを覚えている。パリッと歯切れがよく、適度な厚みがあって丈夫なことに加えて、とろけるような口どけと香ばしい甘みも欠かせない。これらの条件を満たすのが、築地「丸山海苔店」の"こんとび"だ。この海苔は黒い海苔に青海苔が点々と混ざるのが特徴。青海苔の野趣溢れる香りは昔の海苔に近い。こんとびの名前は、「混」「飛」という青海苔が混ざった海苔の等級に由来しているという。同じこんとびでも青海苔の混ざり具合で風味は変わり、黒光りして青海苔がはっきり飛んだものを特注している。保存は丸山海苔店オリジナルの乾燥剤を入れ真空パックしてから密閉容器へ。海苔を取ることを「手繰る」と言うが、営業中は手の湿っていない人が手繰り、徹底して湿気を防ぐ。海苔巻を切るときは刃の角度を70度に傾けると、パリリと香ばしい音が響く。これも鮨を旨くする技の一つだ。

Nori is sushi's famous support act, co-starring frequently as everything from hosomaki and futomaki rolls to gunkan-maki and the strips around nigiri. When making your selection, the first important thing is the fragrance. In my father's day, six months' worth of nori was kept in a tea chest at home, and I vividly recall the suffocating seaweed smell in that room. Nori has to be crispy, robust, just the right thickness, and simultaneously melt-in-the-mouth and fragrantly sweet. "Kontobi" nori from the Maruyama Nori store in Tsukiji, distinguished by its sprinkling of aonori (green nori) among the black ticks all these boxes. The rustic aroma of the aonori recalls the nori of old. The name Kontobi apparently comes from the grade of nori that contains aonori, and I have a standing order for that of glistening black, with clear specks of aonori, which I store in a vacuum pack with Maruyama's own original desiccant, in a sealed container, to be handled during opening hours only by those without damp hands, to keep out moisture. When cutting norimaki, hold the blade at a 70-degree angle to produce that tantalizing crisp sound: yet another technique for tastier sushi.

nori

山葵
(wasabi)

新緑を思わせる黄緑の美しい色味とツンと鼻に抜ける辛さが山葵の持ち味。爽やかな風味は絶妙なアクセントになり、魚の甘みを鮮明にしてくれる。鮨の薬味に使い始めたのは江戸後期といわれるが、冷蔵庫がなかった時代には、その殺菌作用が果たす役割も大きかっただろう。山葵を挟めばネタとシャリの密着度も増す。「サビ抜きはいつも以上に真剣に握らないと恥をかく」とは父の言葉だ。山葵の品種には大きく"実生"と"真妻"があり、使うのは後者だ。葉の付け根が赤味を帯び、濃い緑の根茎は硬くて緻密。粘りが強く、上品な甘みを備えている。仕入れるのは2年物。脂が乗った秋・冬の魚には辛みが強い静岡の中伊豆や御殿場のものを、春・夏のさっぱりとした魚には香りの高い長野・安曇野産が合う。おろす道具は銅のおろし金一筋だ。鮫皮はおろし方がワンパターンだが、おろし金は表裏で目の粗さが違い、さらに目の一部を叩いて潰しているので多様なおろし方ができる。保存はキッチンペーパーに包んで、産地から取り寄せた沢の水をかけて冷蔵庫にしまう。文字通り"水が合う"のか、鮮度を保ちやすい気がする。

Wasabi is characterized by its pea-green, new-leaf coloring, and that distinctive, heady hit that reverberates through the nasal passages. Its bracing flavor is the perfect accent to the sweetness of fish. First used in sushi in the later Edo period, before refrigeration its antibacterial effect was also doubtless a major reason for its adoption. Wasabi also helps topping and rice adhere to each other, and my father said that making nigiri without it for children was always more difficult to do properly. Broadly speaking there are two varieties of wasabi: mishō and mazuma, and I use the latter, which has a reddish tinge where the leaves attach, and a dark green root that is hard and compact. Mazuma is sticky, with a refined sweetness. I use hotter wasabi from Nakaizu and Gotenba in Shizuoka for the fattier fish of autumn and winter, and more fragrant wasabi from Azumino in Nagano for lighter-tasting spring/summer fish. I use two-year-old roots and a copper grater with a different grain back and front, and part of the grain flattened, allowing various types of grating. To store, wrap the wasabi in kitchen paper and splash on water from the stream the root grew in before refrigerating. This does seem to help it stay fresh for longer.

wasabi

生姜

(shōga)

生姜の甘酢漬けを"ガリ"と呼ぶのは鮨屋の符牒。ガリガリとした食感や生姜を削るときの音に由来するらしい。甘酸っぱさと爽快な辛みは口直しに最適だ。握りの合間につまめば舌がリセットされ、次の1貫の味が鮮明になる。もともとは生魚で冷えた胃腸の調子を整える意味もあったようだ。もちろん、ガリは自家製である。使うのは高知産の新生姜。特にゴールデンウィークの頃に出荷される新生姜は歯触りがよく、連休を利用して1年分を仕込んでいる。包丁で芽や皮を取り除いた生姜は、塊のまま塩でよく揉みアクを抜くことが大切だ。ゆがいて水切りしたら、甘酢に漬け込めば出来上がりである。甘酢の材料は、赤酢、水、砂糖、塩。砂糖を少なめにしてすっきりと仕上げている。完成したガリは気温の変動が少ない地下室に保管し、1週間分を鉋で薄く削って使っていく。修業先ではガリの仕込みは若手の仕事。塩負けして赤くなった手が、塩かぶれしなくなったら一人前に近づいた証拠と言われた。店ではつまみから握りに移るタイミングでつけ台に出し、なくなったら補充する。ただし、食べ過ぎるのは野暮というもの。追加は1回程度に留めたい。

In sushi argot ginger pickled in sweet vinegar brine is known as "gari" from its crisp ("gari-gari") texture and the sound made when you shave it. Its sour-sweet taste and bracing bite make it the ideal palate cleanser. Snacking on gari between nigiri resets the taste buds, adding clarity to the next bite of sushi. Originally, it is said, ginger also served to settle a gut chilled by raw fish. I make my own gari, using young ginger from Kōchi. After peeling and cutting off any buds, it is important to rub the ginger root thoroughly with salt to remove any bitterness. Boil briefly, drain and marinate in sweetened vinegar made from akazu (red vinegar), water, sugar and salt. I use less sugar for a sharper finish. Once ready the gari is kept in the basement, where the temperature remains largely constant, and a week's worth planed off at a time. Where I trained prepping the ginger was always the least favorite job, and it was said that you were almost a chef when your salt-ravaged red hands no longer had a rash. I place gari on the counter when moving from tsumami to nigiri, and replenish when it runs out. Scoffing to excess though is uncouth: one extra serving should suffice.

ginger

茶
(cha)

「直接、お金をいただかないものにどれだけよい品を使えるか。店の格はそこから生まれる」。父や修業先の親方に、そう厳しく言われてきた。山葵、海苔、ガリとともに、お茶もその一つだ。理想とするのは、香り高く、甘くまろやかで後口のキレがよいお茶。そのために、煎茶、深蒸し茶、玉露、粉茶、抹茶をブレンドしている。ベースになる煎茶は甘みと深みを出すため、静岡、京都・宇治、宮崎の3産地を配合。濃厚な味わいを生む深蒸し茶は鹿児島の知覧茶、旨みのもとになる玉露はほんのり潮の香りがする宮崎産の海沿いの地域の品を選んでいる。色とコクを生む粉茶は埼玉の狭山茶、まろやかさを出す抹茶は宇治の薄茶だ。すべてミキサーで粉にし、茶漉しで抽出する。温度は差し替えの度に徐々に高くし、締めに出すお茶を最も熱くして口に残った魚や酒の香りを流して帰っていただく。それが江戸前の流儀だと教わった。最後に出すお茶がいわゆる"上がり"で、会計やタクシーを呼ぶといった帰り支度をする意味合いも含んでいる。いずれにせよ、お茶は握りに最も合う飲み物。酒はつまみと楽しんで、握りはお茶で味わってほしいとさえ思う。

My father and former bosses told me in no uncertain terms that a sushi restaurant's standing depended on using the finest products for items not directly chargeable to the customer. Alongside wasabi, nori and gari, tea is one such item. The ideal tea is fragrant, sweet and smooth, with a clean finish. To achieve this I blend a sencha base from Shizuoka, Uji and Miyazaki teas; Chiran tea from Kagoshima for intense fukamushi-cha flavor; umami-rich gyokuro from the Miyazaki coast for a whiff of brine; powdered tea from Sayama, Saitama for color and depth, and Uji usucha for the mellow matcha component, then pulverize the lot in a blender, and brew using a tea strainer. With each refill I gradually raise the temperature, serving the hottest tea to finish to wash away any lingering fish flavor or sake before the customer departs, as I was taught was Edomae custom. The final tea served is called the "agari" and also signals preparations for departure are underway, such as calculating the bill and calling a taxi. In any case, tea is the beverage that suits nigiri best, to the extent that ideally, one would enjoy alcohol with tsumami, and tea with nigiri.

tea

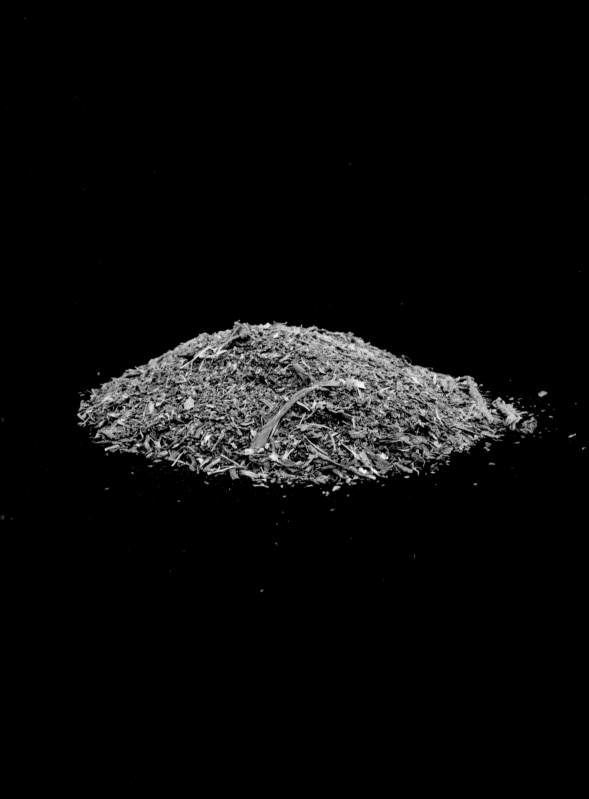

絶品・佳品
zeppin/kahin (delicacies/rarities)

蒸し鮑肝のせ

(mushi-awabi-kimo-nose)

年の瀬が近づくとつまみに加わるのがこの品だ。使うのは冬が旬の蝦夷鮑。名前の通り、主に北海道や東北地方の岩礁域に生息するこぶりの鮑だ。三陸・宮城産の品質がよく、もっぱらこれを仕入れている。蒸し方は夏に獲れる眼高鮑と同様、まずは殻のままたっぷりの塩をかけて身を引き締めることが欠かせない。暴れる鮑が落ち着くのを待ってから、塩を洗い落として殻から外す。身についた汚れをタワシでよく洗ったら、肝と一緒に殻に戻して酒を振りかけて3時間ほどじっくりと蒸していく。このとき1時間おきに酒をかけるのがしっとり仕上げるコツだ。蒸し上がったらそのまま蒸し器におき、粗熱が取れたら下のバットに溜まった蒸し汁をボウルにあけ、その中に身と肝を浸けて冷蔵庫で保存する。店で出すときは必ず常温に戻し、切りつけた上に肝をのせる。塩と山葵を添えるが、なにもつけなくても十分。身はしっとり柔らかく、噛む度に澄んだ旨みが溢れ出す。ねっとりとした肝を一緒に頬張れば、ソースの代わりになる。この蒸し鮑は1人1個をつけ、たっぷりと召し上がっていただくのが常。暮れの時季にふさわしい贅沢な一品だ。

As the year draws to a close, this dish joins the tsumami menu. I use winter's Ezo abalone, a small species found on rocky shores mainly in Hokkaidō (Ezo being the old name for the lands north of Honshū), and Tōhoku, sourcing it exclusively from Miyagi due to the excellent quality. Like summer's madaka abalone, always start by sprinkling generously with salt while in the shell to firm the flesh. Once the agitated abalone has settled, rinse off salt and remove from shell. Scrub off any detritus, then return flesh to shell with liver, sprinkle over sake and steam slowly for about three hours. The trick to succulent results is to sprinkle on more sake every hour. When done, leave in the steamer to cool slightly, then drain juices accumulated in the tray into a bowl, add flesh and liver and refrigerate. Return to room temperature to serve, cutting the flesh and placing liver on top. The abalone is served with salt and wasabi, but really requires no seasoning. The flesh will be soft and juicy, unalloyed umami exploding in the mouth with every bite. Chewed with the flesh, the sticky liver will serve as sauce. I usually allow one of these luxurious steamed abalone per person.

steamed abalone with its liver

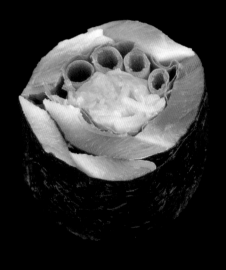

〆鯖 磯辺巻

(shime-saba isobemaki)

お任せのコースの内容は来店する方の希望に沿って決めるが、つまみを3〜4品出してから握りに進むことが多い。そのつまみの1品によくつくるのが〆鯖の磯辺巻である。海苔の上に〆鯖を7切れ並べ、大葉、あさつき、薄切りのガリをのせて簾できゅっと巻けば出来上がりだ。この磯辺巻の魅力は切り口の美しさにある。黒々とした海苔の中から淡く紅白に色づく〆鯖が顔をのぞかせ、その間をガリの桃色とあさつきや大葉の鮮やかな緑が彩る。カウンターが華やぐほど艶やかだ。味の組み合わせも絶妙だ。脂の乗った鯖の濃厚な旨みを堪能させつつ、ガリの甘酸っぱさや大葉の爽やかな香味によってさっぱりと食べられる。海苔の香ばしさもよく合い、光物があまり得意ではない人にも喜んでいただける。よい鯖が手に入らない時季は、〆た鯵や鰯でつくることもあり、それもまた旨い。そもそも塩と酢で魚を〆るのは鮨屋の古い仕事だが、それにガリを合わせて海苔で巻くところがいかにも江戸前らしく、個人的にも好きなつまみの一つだ。これを覚えたのは修業先である「なか田」。これからも残していきたい老舗の伝統を受け継ぐ一品だ。

One appetizer I often make of the 3-4 generally served before proceeding to nigiri. Simply arrange seven pieces of mackerel on a sheet of nori, top with ōba (green shiso), asatsuki chives, and thin strips of gari (sushi ginger), and use a mat to roll tightly. The cut face of this isobemaki is a big part of its charm: the red-and-white tinged mackerel peeking out from among the black of the nori, the spectacle completed by the pink of the gari and vibrant green of the ōba and chives in a vibrant display that lights up the counter. The flavor combination is just as exquisite; the intense umami of the fatty mackerel showcased by the sour-sweet tang of the ginger and fresh fragrance of the ōba. The fragrant nori is also a perfect fit in this dish to delight even those less enamored of oilier fish. Just as tasty with cured aji or sardines if good mackerel is unavailable. Curing fish with salt and vinegar is a time-honored sushi chef task, but combining it with gari and wrapping in nori is quintessential Edomae, and also one of my own favorite tsumami. I learned to make this while training at Nakata in the Imperial Hotel, and it's a venerable tradition well worth keeping.

shime-saba (cured mackerel) isobemaki

小肌の木の葉造り

(kohada-no-konohazukuri)

塩と酢でキリッと〆る小肌は、握りにして味が引き立つネタの代表といえるだろう。お造りとして出すことは滅多にないが、ひと手間加えることによって酒を呼ぶ一品になる。木の葉造りはその好例だ。1人前に使うのは小肌2尾分。それぞれ身のほうに山葵、刻んだガリ、胡麻を挟み、三等分にしてから切り口を見せるように盛り付ける。木の葉を模した見た目は小粋な印象があり、小肌、ガリ、山葵という組み合わせも鮨屋ならではといえる。店の特徴も出やすいため、先付にすることが多い。小肌好きにはとりわけ喜ばれるつまみである。この品を広めた店としては、神田・神保町の「鶴八」が有名だ。ただし、比較的ポピュラーな鮨屋のつまみでもあり、最初に修業した神田「三亀鮨」でもよく出していた。父も駆け出しの頃、この店でお世話になっていたため、小肌の木の葉造りを好んでつくっていたことを覚えている。ちなみに、木の葉造りとは刺身の盛り付けの一つの技法でもあり、細魚や秋刀魚などにも用いられる。伝統的なその技を応用して、鮨屋らしい気の利いた酒肴に仕立てたのは、まさに先人の知恵といえるだろう。

Piquant salt-and-vinegar cured kohada (gizzard shad) is perhaps the best-known example of a topping enhanced by use in nigiri. Though rarely served as sashimi, with minimal effort it makes a perfect accompaniment to drinks, especially presented in this leaf-pattern style. Allow two kohada per person. Sandwich wasabi, grated gari and sesame between the kohada flesh, cut into three equal pieces, and arrange with the cut surface upward. The leaf pattern is a stylish touch, and the kohada-gari-wasabi combo a typical sushi chef creation. An easy way to set one's restaurant apart, it is often served as an appetizer, and is a huge hit with kohada fans. Tsuruhachi in Kanda Jinbōchō is famous for this dish, but it is actually a fairly popular sushi tsumami also served at Mikamezushi in Kanda where I started training. Mikamezushi also helped my father when he was starting out, so this kohada sashimi dish was a favorite item of his. Arranging in a leaf pattern is a recognized sashimi technique also used for the likes of sayori and sanma, and thanks to our forebears' expertise, we can still apply this traditional skill to make an attractive tsumami perfect for a sushi restaurant.

leaf-pattern kohada sashimi

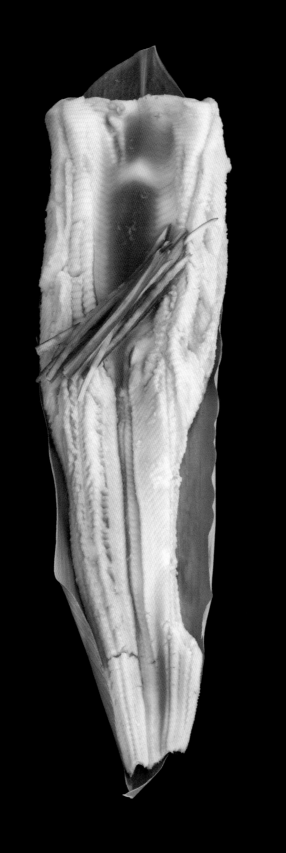

炙り穴子
(aburi-anago)

穴子は一年中切らすことのない定番の鮨ネタだが、この炙り穴子を出すのは毎年7月3日頃から7日まで。五節句の一つである七夕にちなんだ季節限定の酒肴である。これを覚えたのは「なか田」での修業時代。用意するのは笹飾りになぞらえた隈笹の葉だ。短冊を吊るす笹よりも大きく厚みもあるので、穴子を載せて炙るのに適している。ちなみに、隈笹は盛り込みの仕切りとしても古くから使われてきた。彩りになるのはもちろん、ネタの匂い移りを防いだり、乾燥から守ったり、鮮度を保持したりとさまざまに役立ち、鮨との縁は深い。一方、穴子はこの時季、ちょうど産卵前にあたり旬の真っ盛りだ。握りのネタと同様、1時間以上かけてふっくらと煮上げたものを使う。隈笹の上に置いたら遠火の中火で焦げないようにゆっくりと炙り、清涼感のある香ばしい香りをふわりと軽く纏わせる。炙った穴子は笹に載せたまま出すのが習わしだ。川に浮かぶ笹舟のような風流な姿も味のうちというわけである。「ああ、もうすぐ七夕か」「雨が降らないといいですね」。カウンター越しに交わされるそんなやりとりもまた、夏の到来を告げる風物詩になっている。

Anago is a sushi staple kept on hand through the year, but I only serve this particular dish, which I learned to make during my time at Nakata, from around the 3rd to 7th of July, for Tanabata, one of Japan's five seasonal festivals. I start by obtaining leaves of kuma bamboo grass to mimic the bamboo grass decorations of the season. These are larger and thicker than the bamboo grass used for hanging wishes on paper strips at this time of year, so form a suitable base for the anago. Kuma bamboo grass has a long association with sushi, in its capacity as a serving divider not only acting as a decoration but also stopping the transfer of odors, and keeping food moist and fresh. Anago meanwhile is at its finest at this time, just prior to spawning. Use eel that has been boiled to fluffy tenderness for at least an hour, as for nigiri. Place on leaves and grill slowly on medium heat, not too close to the flame (to avoid charring), to impart an invigorating, fragrant aroma. The usual custom is to serve on the leaves, the air of bamboo-leaf boat on a river adding to the flavor. Chat across the counter about Tanabata and the weather is another harbinger of summer.

seared anago (conger eel)

唐墨と雲丹の塩辛
(karasumi and uni shiokara)

唐墨は年の瀬の味覚である。12月中旬から大晦日まで、お通しに出すのが恒例だ。仕込むのは、10月上旬から11月にかけて。鰡子と呼ばれる鰡の卵巣が市場に並び始めたらスタートとなる。大きなものほど味がよいため、長崎など九州産を仕入れることが多い。鰡は成長に伴って名前が変わる出世魚であり、鰡よりも大きい鯔から取った卵が最適である。唐墨づくりは、血抜き、塩漬け、塩出し、酒漬け、干しといくつもの工程があり、1ヵ月は優にかかる。さらに、店では干した後、アクや匂いを取るため軽く味噌漬けにするので、一般的な唐墨よりも茶色がかった色合いに仕上がる。日本三大珍味に挙がるだけあり、チーズに似た独特の旨みとねっとりとした舌触りが酒を呼ぶ。この唐墨と一緒に出すのが雲丹の塩辛である。これには宮崎の赤雲丹がよく合う。1粒ずつペーパーに並べた雲丹に塩を打って水分を抜いていく。このとき、アクが戻らないようこまめに下紙を替えることが大切だ。3時間ほどおき、最後に浮き出た水分を拭き取れば完成である。箸先にほんの少し載せて日本酒とともに味わえば、師走の慌ただしさを忘れる風雅な時間が訪れる。

Karasumi is a year-end treat, commonly served as an appetizer from mid-December to New Year's Eve, and prepared from early October through to November, when the roe of bora (mullet) starts to appear on the market. The bigger the sac the better in terms of taste, so I tend to use that from Kyūshū. Larger bora are known as dodo, and provide the most suitable roe. There are several steps in making karasumi—bleeding, marinating in brine, desalinating, marinating in sake, and drying—that together take easily a month. After drying we then pickle the roe lightly in miso to expunge any fishy odor or taste, producing a karasumi browner than most. The distinctive cheesy umami and sticky mouthfeel that give karasumi its status as one of Japan's top three delicacies do indeed call for a drink. Served alongside is uni shiokara, aka-uni from Miyazaki being a good match. Line up uni on paper and salt to remove moisture, remembering to change the paper to stop the fishiness returning. Leave for about three hours, and wipe off water to finish. Take a little on the tips of your chopsticks to consume with sake, and enjoy an indulgent break from the year-end rush.

mullet roe and sea urchin shiokara

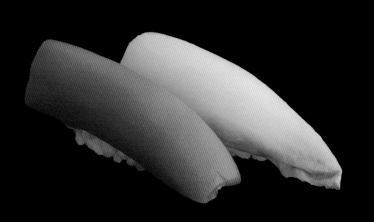

パプリカ・チコリ

(papurika and chikori)

鮨の主役は魚である。魚を味わうための料理といっても過言ではない。ところが、あるとき来店した方は連れの1人がベジタリアンで、魚を食べられないという。「なにも出さなくていい」と言われたものの、せっかくいらしたのだから一緒に楽しんでいただきたい。そこで頭を捻って考えたのが、魚に見立てた野菜の握りである。たとえば、鮪の赤身に代わるのは肉厚の赤いパプリカ。湯引きして皮を剥き、昆布だしに浸け込んでから握る。真紅の色味ととろんとした口当たりは、かなり赤身に近い。白身の代わりに選んだのはチコリだ。これもやはり昆布だしで柔らかく煮ると、見た目も食感も白身もどきになる。他にも、エリンギ茸はだしで煮てから昆布〆にすると鮑に近い味わいになることや、舞茸はつぶ貝の代わりになるといった発見もあった。これらにアスパラの握り、芽ねぎやスプラウトの軍艦巻などを加えて、同席された方と同じ数の握りを出すことができた。もちろん、野菜を握ろうと思えたのは、シャリとの相性など味の点でも納得できたことが大きい。鮨屋で味わってほしいのは魚だが、グローバル時代にはこうした工夫も必要になるのだろう。

Fish is sushi's star turn, but I did once have a vegetarian customer turn up, and as they had made the effort to come, I felt they should enjoy themselves as much as everyone else. Wracking my brains, I came up with vegetable nigiri resembling fish. For red fleshy tuna, I substituted fleshy red bell pepper that had been blanched, peeled, and marinated in kombu dashi before making into nigiri. The bright red coloring and heavy mouthfeel were quite close to red meat. For white fish, I chose chicory. This resembles white fish in both appearance and texture when simmered until tender in kombu dashi. I also discovered that eringi mushrooms simmered in dashi then kombu-cured taste a lot like abalone, while maitake mushrooms serve as whelks. Adding asparagus nigiri and gunkanmaki of green onion shoots or sprouts, I was able to serve the vegetarian customer the same number of nigiri as their dining companion. Naturally, how the vegetable will complement the rice and other flavor considerations are big factors in successful vegetarian nigiri. A sushi restaurant is a place to savor seafood, but sometimes the global era we live in demands a little more inventiveness.

capsicum and chicory

帆立黄身酢掛け
(hotate kimisugake)

このつまみをつくるのは、北海道・野付の帆立貝が入荷する12月から4月頃まで。天然物の大きな帆立貝があってこその一品だ。ポイントは下に敷いた菜の花。見た目の華やかさだけでなく、寒さ厳しい季節に春の息吹を感じていただきたいという思いを込めている。着想を得たのは京都の料亭だ。鯛のお造りに菜の花が敷いてあり、その美しさに目を奪われた。帆立貝にも合うと直感したが、もうひと捻りを加えたいと黄身酢掛けにした。卵黄、酢、砂糖を湯煎にかけてつくる黄身酢は、とろりまろやかで甘酸っぱい合わせ酢だ。これが野付の帆立貝の濃厚な甘みと菜の花のほろ苦さを軽やかにつなぎ、バランスの取れた味わいになる。他にも、野付の帆立貝を使ったつまみには卵白で泡立てただし醤油掛けもあり、こちらもまた人気が高い。これらの品をつくるまで、貝柱のつまみは山葵醤油で出すのみだった。しかし、日本酒やワインをオーダーする方は9割以上。手を掛けた品で酒を楽しんでほしいと趣向を凝らすようになったのである。父親世代の鮨職人には「バカなことをしている」と一笑に付されるかもしれないが、お客様の満足度を第一にしたい。

I prepare this tsumami from December to April when large wild scallops ship from Notsuke in Hokkaidō. The rape blossom (nanohana) base is key: not only for its colorful appearance, but for the whiff of spring it brings at the coldest time of year. Inspired by a ryōtei in Kyōto, where rape blossom was laid on seabream sashimi to stunning effect, intuitively it seemed a good fit for scallops, but I added kimisu dressing for an extra twist. Made by mixing egg yolk, vinegar and sugar in a bowl in hot water, kimisu is a thick, rich, tangy condiment that effortlessly joins the intense sweetness of the scallops and bittersweet rape blossom in a perfectly-balanced gustatory sensation. Another popular scallop tsumami features stock-suffused shōyu containing egg white for foaming. I used to simply serve shellfish adductors with wasabi and shōyu, but nine out of ten customers order sake or wine, so I wanted to offer them something more sophisticated in the snack department. Sushi chefs of my father's generation would probably dismiss this as a waste of time, but for me, it's all about satisfying the customer.

scallop with kimisu

INDEX

握りについて：左頁に掲載の握りは前頁に、
右頁に掲載の握りは次頁に解説しています。

Nigiri spreads: Nigiri appearing on left-hand pages are described on the previous spread, and those shown on the right, the spread to follow.

坂西誠一 (さかにし せいいち)

1962年東京生まれ。1980年高校卒業後、神田三亀鮨に入店。その後、帝国ホテルの江戸前寿司なか田で修業。1993年実家の国分寺都寿司の二代目となる。現在は、店舗を駅前から静かな住宅地に移し、予約限定の寿司店を妻の利枝子と共に生業としている。

Seiichi Sakanishi

Born 1962 in Tokyo. After graduating high school in 1980, Sakanishi joined the staff of Mikame-zushi in Kanda, and trained thereafter at the Imperial Hotel's Edomae Sushi Nakata. In 1993, he succeeded his father as second-generation owner-chef of Miyako-zushi in Kokubunji. He has since moved the restaurant from the station district to a private house in a quiet residential area, where he runs the sushi shop together with his wife, Rieko, on a by-reservation-only basis.

田島一彦 (たじま かずひこ)

1946年東京生まれ。1969年多摩美術大学デザイン科卒業後、資生堂宣伝部入社。2005年同社部長クリエイティブディレクターを経て独立、現在フリー。受賞歴：朝日広告賞、毎日広告賞、読売広告賞、フジサンケイ広告大賞、日経広告賞、電通賞、ACC賞、日本雑誌広告賞、ニューヨークフェスティバル等。『江戸花図鑑』『江戸鳥図鑑』『江戸魚図鑑』（すべてパイ インターナショナル）

Kazuhiko Tajima

Born 1946 in Tokyo. Graduated in design from Tama Art University in 1969. After working in the advertising department of Shiseido, eventually as creative director, Tajima began working as an independent art director in 2005. Among his many awards are the Asahi Advertising Award, Mainichi Advertisement Design Award, Yomiuri Advertising Award, Fuji Sankei Advertising Award, Nikkei Advertising Award, Dentsu Award, ACC Award, Japan Magazine Advertising Award, and New York Festival Award.

与田弘志 (よだ ひろし)

1942年東京生まれ。イギリスの美術学校及び David Montgomery Studio で写真を学び、1966年ファッション写真家として独立。ロンドンに Hiroshi Studio を設立し、エディトリアルを中心に活動。1972年東京に本拠を移し、雑誌.企業広告で写真を発表。講談社出版文化賞、東京ADC最高賞、毎日広告賞最高賞など受賞。国内外で多くの写真展を開催。写真集『TEA FOR TWO』『OBSESSION』『和菓子』（PIE BOOKS） www.hiroshiyoda.com

Hiroshi Yoda

Born 1942 in Tokyo. Studied photography at art schools in the UK and the David Montgomery Studio. Yoda launched his career as a fashion photographer in 1966, when he established the Hiroshi Studio in London, working primarily in editorial photography. He relocated to Tokyo in 1972. His photographs appear in magazines and corporate advertising. He is recipient of the Kodansha Publication Culture Awards for Photography, Tokyo ADC Award Grand Prize, and Mainichi Advertising Design Award Grand Prize, among others. His published books include the photo collections *Tea for Two* and *Obsession*, and with PIE Books, *Wagashi*. www.hiroshiyoda.com

鮨ネタ 粋ワザ

Sushi Revealed:Secrets of a Japanese Chef

2022年5月2日　初版第1刷発行

文　坂西誠一
企画・アートディレクション　田島一彦
写真　与田弘志

取材　上島寿子
翻訳　パメラ ミキ / カーステン マクアイヴァー
デザイン　淡海季史子
校正　鷗来堂
編集　高橋かおる

発行人　三芳寛要
発行元　株式会社 パイ インターナショナル
〒170-0005　東京都豊島区南大塚2-32-4
TEL 03-3944-3981 FAX 03-5395-4830
sales@pie.co.jp

印刷・製本　株式会社広済堂ネクスト

text©2022 Seiichi Sakanishi
design©2022 Kazuhiko Tajima
photographs@2022 Hiroshi Yoda
©2022 PIE International

ISBN978-4-7562-5608-9 C0077
Printed in Japan